VOLCANO

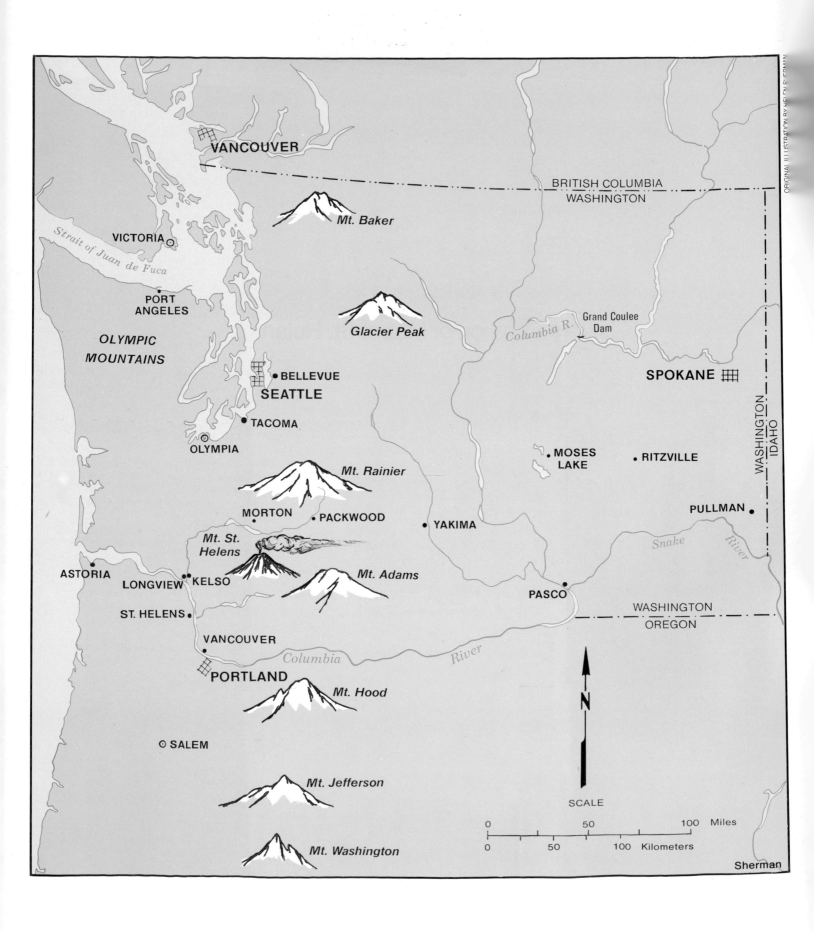

VANCOUVER

BRITISH COLUMBIA
WASHINGTON

Mt. Baker

VICTORIA ⊙

Strait of Juan de Fuca

PORT
ANGELES

Glacier Peak

Columbia R.

Grand Coulee
Dam

OLYMPIC
MOUNTAINS

BELLEVUE

SPOKANE ⊞

SEATTLE

WASHINGTON
IDAHO

TACOMA

OLYMPIA ⊙

• MOSES
LAKE

• RITZVILLE

Mt. Rainier

MORTON • PACKWOOD • YAKIMA

PULLMAN •

*Mt. St.
Helens*

Mt. Adams

Snake

River

ASTORIA

LONGVIEW • KELSO

ST. HELENS

PASCO

WASHINGTON
OREGON

VANCOUVER

Columbia

River

N

PORTLAND

Mt. Hood

⊙ SALEM

SCALE

Mt. Jefferson

| 0 | | 50 | | 100 | Miles |

| 0 | 50 | 100 | Kilometers |

Mt. Washington

Sherman

VOLCANO

The Eruption of Mount St. Helens

Written and edited by the combined staffs of

The Daily News, Longview, Washington

and

The Journal-American, Bellevue, Washington

Longview Publishing Company • Longview, Washington

Madrona Publishers • Seattle

IN CANADA

Douglas and McIntyre, Vancouver

VOLCANO

The Eruption of Mount St. Helens

A Briefing on a Dynamite Keg

He had looked like a fearless lumberjack, his left hand clutching the stocking cap that covered his blond hair, his face in a grimace, squinting at the mountain. A small group of reporters, their eyes darting nervously upward at the peak, huddled around him. They were all standing in a parking lot 4,300 feet up the north side of Mount St. Helens. It was March 27, 1980.

That day, three hours earlier, the mountain had belched steam and ash. It was waking up after 123 years, and David Johnston (in photograph at right), the lumberjack-looking geologist, was telling them why—and more.

"It is extremely dangerous where we are standing," he said evenly. "If the mountain exploded, we would die. It's like standing next to a dynamite keg with the fuse lit. Only we don't know how long that fuse is."

The reporters stared at him. Johnston, 30, an expert from the federal government's Geological Survey, was giving a briefing in the field. The ground kept shaking.

If the mountain does blow, Johnston told them, it's not the lava they should be afraid of. It's the mudflows, rivers of ash and melting snow that could devastate the beautiful river valleys spread out for miles below. It's the avalanches of hot ash and gas—pyroclastic flows—that could sear Mount St. Helens' slopes and anyone or anything they touched.

Still, in spite of the danger, they were all stand-

ing there. The peril, simply, was not to be believed.

In fact, in March of 1980, and in April and into May, not many people in Washington believed Mount St. Helens would erupt. Volcanoes were in faraway places, in newspapers and magazines. Eruptions happened in South America, in Italy, in the South Seas and in the movies—and then only on the late, late show.

For people in Washington, the majestic mountains served as backdrops for photos, heights to be conquered with pitons and belays. They were quiet, snow-covered giants—perfect for postcards, essential for skiing, and nice to look at when you sat in a rowboat waiting for the trout to bite.

But David Johnston knew them as volcanoes, a subject he had studied all of his adult life.

His enthusiasm had nearly killed him once. He had been trapped on an island near Mount Augustine in Alaska in 1976 and was plucked to safety only hours before the mountain erupted.

And yet, now he could not leave Mount St. Helens. By early May, scientists were worried that the camp where Johnston and other government geologists were working might be inundated by snow and ice slides. The camp was moved five miles away to a ridge directly north of the mountain. The experts said that would be safe.

Since the day in March when Johnston talked to reporters, a bulge of rock and ice had been growing on the north face of the mountain at an astounding five feet a day. Geologists had warned that an enormous amount of pressure could be building under that bulge. But they weren't sure. They said it might blow, but they didn't know when, if ever. Mount St. Helens was giving them few clues.

David Johnston was up at about sunrise on May 18, a Sunday. He was alone in the camp. Everything was quiet.

The night before he had radioed fellow scientists in Vancouver, Washington, 40 miles away to the southwest, that there was nothing new to

report. Already that morning he had radioed again, saying the same thing. All was well.

The bulge on the north side of the mountain was now a half-mile long and had puffed out like a 500-foot boil. It was right in front of him.

Suddenly the ground shook.

Johnston's eyes shot toward the mountain. It shook again. He clutched his radio transmitter. He was shouting.

Vancouver never heard him; the transmission was somehow blocked. A ham radio operator, the only one who did hear Johnston, said he hadn't sounded frightened. Instead, he had sounded excited. It was 8:32 a.m.

"Vancouver! Vancouver!" Johnston shouted into the radio.

"This is it . . ."

Viewed from the north, a dormant Mount St. Helens, its beauty mirrored in Spirit Lake, seemed the state's most benign peak.

Following pages: Seen from the air, the once-calm St. Helens vents its deadly volcanic force skyward during the height of its May 18 eruption.

In their minds, Spirit Lake regulars remember this – canoes, calm water, and a St. Helens backdrop.

In a 1960's photograph to promote Spirit Lake tourism, the state showed its clear – if always chilly – waters.

A Place of Beauty and Solace

A cold splash of Spirit Lake's water made your face tingle. A dive in—and the dash back out—was enough to change most people's minds about a long swim on a warm day.

Among the few regular swimmers were the daredevil kids at the YMCA camp on the north shore. From a lakeside seat on a log or a stump, you could watch their water games just offshore, and beyond them an expanse of blue several shades darker than the sky. From the opposite shore, Douglas fir, hemlock and spruce—uncut, centuries-old trees, some several feet thick and 200 feet tall—rose to cover the low hills. The green almost glowed in the sunshine.

Straight south was the mountain. Just five miles away, Mount St. Helens towered, rising above timberline, a great snow mountain standing alone.

Wind blowing off its slopes chilled the nostrils. In calmer air, a pine scent lingered. Streams rolled from the base of the mountain, rippling over rocks and silt in shallows where fishermen waded. A ribbon of highway was strung through one valley, winding westward from the base.

Backpackers left the road to camp near the mountain and fish at any of several small lakes that held brown trout and crayfish. Foot trails in the hills crossed the meadows, the pumice-covered slopes and dense woods, where the giant trees cast a cool shade and the carpet of decaying pine needles grew thick as a sponge. Rain and snow, more common than sunshine in fall, winter and spring, turned the sponge to slush—or hid it under a few inches of whiteness.

Tracks of animals—deer, elk, goats as well as humans—occasionally wove through the trees. Steep trails led to hilltops, where the climb paid off with a view of the mountain. Its gentle slopes made Mount St. Helens look like a symmetrical snowdrift. "The Fujiyama of America," it was called, a calendar photographer's dream.

A Yakima Indian legend explained its beauty and solitude. The peak had once been a toothless old woman in the form of a mountain, named Loo-Wit. The Great Spirit had posted her to guard The Bridge of the Gods across the Columbia River, and to keep peace between two angry, male mountains on opposite sides of the river.

But the two men—brothers named Wyeast and Pahto—feuded, pelting each other with white-hot stones. Some stones shattered the bridge and badly burned and battered Loo-Wit. The Great Spirit heard her moaning and rewarded her by giving her the appearance of a lovely young maiden.

In those pre-dawn moments, standing against the sun, St. Helens brought a sense of awe to its admirers.

But inside she was old—older than Wyeast, which came to be called Mount Hood, and than Pahto, which became Mount Adams. (In geological fact, St. Helens is younger than either.) Loo-Wit's, family and friends had died, so she stood alone and serene in her quiet forest.

Klickitat Indians had a different version of the legend. And they had another name for Mount St. Helens—Tah-one-lat-clah, or Fire Mountain.

And so the peak had stood throughout the white man's coming, while cities and roads were built around her. She watched over not a bridge, but a vacation haven. Visitors to her wilderness left their traffic jams, televisions and eight-to-five jobs behind to experience the outdoors.

St. Helens' slopes were popular with climbers eager for a challenge. Her forests offered freedom from the urban cage. Her lakes and streams let anglers catch their dinners. People who ventured into the woods or onto the mountain knew they were at the mercy of the forces of nature. If it rained, or snowed, or froze or blew at night, they were prepared.

And they were philosophical about it. They knew those elements, the forces of nature that could be so pleasant or so brutal, had shaped and nurtured this majestic wilderness. To the visitors who returned to it year after year, it seemed as if those forces would keep the place sublime forever.

St. Helens: Born of Fire

Rising thousands of feet above the forest-ed hillsides surrounding her, Mount St. Helens was the white-capped monarch of all she surveyed.

But her glistening, snow-clad slopes concealed a fiery genesis. St. Helens and her Cascade Range sisters—Lassen, Shasta, Hood, Rainier and Baker—are part of a chain of volcanoes stretching from northern California to southern British Columbia, just one part of what geologists call the "Pacific Ring of Fire."

It is in this coastal strip—rimming the Pacific from the tip of South America to Alaska, then south through Japan to New Zealand—where the great slabs of the earth's crust meet.

Scientists believe that the tremendous pressure generated by the slabs rubbing together

In this illustration, an oceanic plate rubs against a continental plate, generating incredible heat and pressure, which in turn forms molten rock, or magma. The movement of the Pacific plate has created the so-called "Ring of Fire," a series of volcanoes stretching from Japan to New Zealand, and from Alaska to South America. Typically, the magma works its way up to the surface, and a volcano is born—or rekindled.

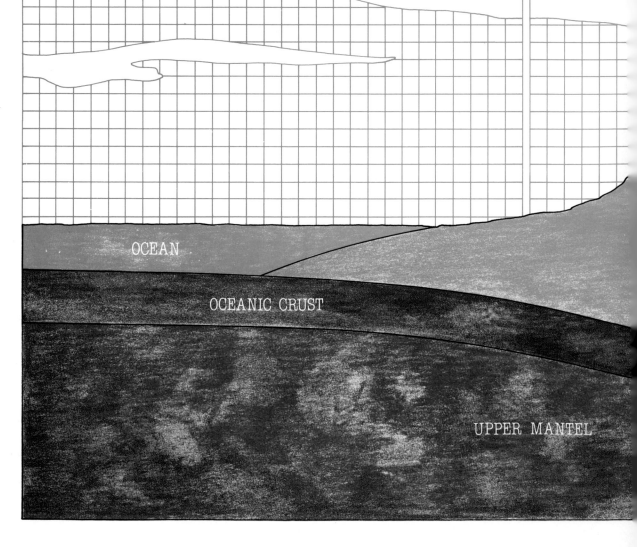

OCEAN

OCEANIC CRUST

UPPER MANTEL

creates pockets of molten rock, called magma.

Lighter than the rock that surrounds it, the magma begins to work its way to the surface. When it does, a volcano is born.

Volcanic eruptions are rare events on the human time scale, but on the geologic clock, which is measured in hundreds of millions of years, they are mere routine ticks. Although some Cascade volcanoes date back more than one million years, they are all relative newcomers to their surrounding terrain; the Cascade Range on which they are superimposed is about seven million years old.

Among these "late-comers" to the geological scene, St. Helens is a youngster.

The mountain, a composite or "stratovolcano," is made up of alternating layers of lava and fragmented material, and it partially conceals the remnants of an older volcano that scientists date back some 37,000 years. In fact, geologists say much of its visible cone has probably been formed within the last 1,000 years. It is the mountain's frequent activity during the past few thousand years that had geologists convinced it would put on a pyrotechnic display before the century was out.

In 1975, three U.S. Geological Survey scientists wrote that St. Helens has been more active and more violent during the last few thousand years than any volcano in the contiguous United States. (Alaska and Hawaii both have several active volcanoes.)

The geologists noted that St. Helens has probably had catastrophic eruptions like that of Mount Vesuvius in 79 A.D. As evidence, they point to traces of ashfall from previous St. Helens eruptions that have been found from geological testing in eastern Montana and southern Alberta, Canada, as well as the more plentiful deposits that helped form the rich soil of eastern Washington.

The mountain's first well-documented eruption occurred in the 19th century, starting in 1842. One eyewitness to that first episode reported "vast columns of lurid smoke and fire ...which, after attaining a certain elevation, spread out in a line parallel to the...horizon, and presented the appearance of a vast table, supported by immense pillars of convolving flame and smoke." Ash from the initial 1842 eruption carried south and eastward to The Dalles in Oregon, some 65 miles away.

The fireworks continued intermittently for 15 years. The Portland Oregonian newspaper reported in 1854 that St. Helens' crater "has been active for several days past...Clouds of smoke and ashes (are) constantly rising from it. The smoke appears to come up in puffs...There is now more smoke issuing from it than there was (a year ago), which indicates that the volcanic fires are rapidly increasing within the bowels of the majestic mountain."

The peak apparently then quieted for about three years, and the last report of activity was 1857.

After that, the volcano slipped into geological slumber, from which it would not awaken for 123 years.

CONTINENTAL CRUST

MAGMA

ORIGINAL ILLUSTRATION BY PHIL SCHMIDT

The Mountain Stirs

At 3:48 p.m. March 20, 1980, a needle jogged on a seismograph at the University of Washington in Seattle. The same thing happened simultaneously in the U.S. Geological Survey's observatory in Newport, Washington, and at dozens of similar monitoring stations throughout the country.

What the instruments were recording was a "good-sized" but not severe earthquake centered 20 miles north of Mount St. Helens.

No one in the area reported feeling it. The earthquake rated only a six-paragraph wire service story the next day in the Daily News of Longview. It was on the third page of the second section, and mentioned that St. Helens was a "volcanic peak." Between 50,000 and 60,000 quakes are recorded each year, but this one caught the attention of USGS volcanologists. Because of its location, it could mean the volcano was stirring to life for the first time this century.

More quakes rocked the area, and began to increase in frequency. After three days, they were being recorded at the rate of 40 per hour.

Still, the government's scientists were reassuring. The tremors, they said, were centered some three miles below the earth's surface, although they had moved to within a few miles of the mountain itself. "It's just a geological fact that volcanoes burp," said one geologist, adding: "If they were really near the surface, then I'd say get out your helmets."

St. Helens was soon to prove this was more than a case of geological indigestion. Shortly after noon on March 27—just one week after the first earthquake— the volcano heralded its reawakening with a jarring explosion and a plume of ash and steam that spouted four miles into the air.

Although geologists said it was not a "large eruption," officials evacuated areas around the mountain. By late afternoon, the mountain's snow-capped summit had a blemish: a soot-black crater estimated to be 250 feet wide and 60 feet deep.

The volcanic display continued. A sheriff's deputy who was stationed near the volcano that night told of moonlit views of steam and ash eruptions, and pristine snow turned black by ash. "It sounded like combat," he said. "There was crackling, booming, banging, rumbling and growling. It was very interesting—but a little spooky."

In the weeks that followed, continued volcanic activity—venting of ash and steam—gave rise to a lot of human activity, on the ground and in the sky. The USGS moved in a team of scientists and set up shop for what they thought would be a long volcano watch. Local officials prepared broadscale evacuation plans and set up

A wisp of steam (above) in late March testified to the reawakening of a dormant volcano—its snow-capped peak now blemished by a soot-black crater (right) 250 feet wide.

With Mount Adams and the moon as a backdrop (right), St. Helens sends up a dark plume in the fading light of an evening in early May. Ash from regular small eruptions has blackened the mountain's south face. The volcano's activities attracted hundreds of sightseers like the family below, intent on photographing the rare event.

roadblocks on highways leading to the peak. The air space around the mountain became congested with planes carrying scientists, journalists and sightseers.

The eruption—the first in the lower 48 states since Mount Lassen's ash and lava display in northern California in 1914-21—became a certified national media event. Reporters from throughout the country converged on the area, and readers and viewers grappled with the difference between "magma" and "pyroclastic flow."

In the Washington towns nearest to the mountain, Longview and Kelso, the volcano stirred a

certain amount of civic pride. "A small event, like an eruptionette, would be great," the Daily News editorialized. "Lots of smoke, lots of steam, and a modest flow of lava down the northeast side toward the Plains of Abraham that are frequently devastated by avalanches. That would leave her pretty faces toward populated areas untouched..."

Kelso elementary school students wrote some songs in honor of the then-modest 1980 eruption. One of them was to the tune of The Muppet Show theme:

Let's get the lava flowing
It's time to light the sky

Let's get those ashes
*   blowing*
On Mount St. Helens
*   tonight—*
Boom, boom, boom, boom.
The crater's getting
*   wider*
The mud is sliding fast
The earth is shaking
*   harder*
Oh yeah, it's shaking
*   harder*
For the most sensational,
irrigational, geographical,
unpredictable
*   This is the time for Mount*
St. Helens to blow!

It was also the time to make

money with volcano souvenirs, like T-shirts with slogans such as "Mount St. Helens is Hot" and "Survivor, Mount St. Helens Eruption, 1980."

But the carnival atmosphere was tempered with the knowledge that the "survivor" claims could be premature. Scientists began talking about the possibilities of mudflows in the valleys near the mountain, and flooding in lower areas. They placed monitoring equipment on St. Helens that was supposed to give at least a few hours—maybe days—warning of a major eruption.

The USGS issued a bulletin advising local residents to stay indoors if ash started falling. The bulletin also warned motorists driving in valleys radiating out from the volcano to be on the lookout for mudflows "which carry boulders and resemble wet flowing concrete. Mudflows can move faster than you can walk or run, but you can drive a car down a valley faster than a mudflow can travel."

The danger didn't keep the tourists away. It attracted them. Hundreds drove as far as roadblocks and to vantage points to get a view of a volcano in action, even though much of the time it was hidden behind a cloudy veil. After merchants in Cougar, near the base of St. Helens, complained that a roadblock was cutting off their share of volcano tourist business, the barricade was moved north of town—toward the mountain.

The road block on the highway to Spirit Lake became a mecca drawing sightseers from across the nation as well as Germans, Swiss, Canadians and Israelis. "We left Canada at 7 this morning to see the mountain shakin' and blowin'," said one of the campers. "We'll just stay. You only live once, eh what? Never worry until tomorrow."

Some weren't content to do their mountain watching from afar. A 21-year old Washington man climbed the peak April 3, and said he could see the ground moving "like waves on the ocean." He said he smelled the rotten-egg odor of sulfur near the crater, and was showered with an inch of ash.

Some were willing to go beyond the crater's edge. The Cowlitz County sheriff's office received a phone call from Cleveland, Ohio, offering a young woman as a sacrifice to the mountain. "I don't think it would work," deadpanned a deputy. "If we are going to offer a sacrifice, we should use a native." A Boston TV newsman ran an April Fool's Day "bulletin" warning that a nearby ski resort had begun spitting lava and flames. Film of St. Helens interspersed with shots of burning

houses were used to embellish the report—which cost the newsman his job.

As April waned, so did ash and steam eruptions from St. Helens. But the mountain's relative calm was deceptive. Scientists, comparing pictures of the mountain before March 27 with others taken nearly a month later, discovered an ominous bulge at the head of Forsyth Glacier, about 8,000 feet up the north face of the mountain. The area had expanded about 300 feet, and was continuing to grow at the incredible rate of five feet per day. Experts speculated it was caused by the pressure of molten rock moving up within the volcano. But a major eruption didn't seem to concern them as much as the possibility that the glacier, which was described as a "time bomb sitting on marbles," would race down the north slope into Spirit Lake. Some said it would travel as fast as 180 mph.

The Forest Service decided not to let any of its workers go within five miles of the peak. The Boy Scouts cleaned out their camp at Spirit Lake. Washington Governor Dixy Lee Ray set up a "red zone" five miles around the peak, ordering everyone except scientists and law enforcement officers to get out. One resident, an 83-year-old Spirit Lake resort owner with the name of Harry Truman, refused to leave.

Residents of the tiny town of Toutle, 25 miles west of the peak, were told not to panic. Donal Mullineaux, one of three USGS scientists who had predicted in 1975 that St. Helens would erupt before the end of the century, told a meeting of anxious residents a "large event" at the mountain was unlikely. Know the quickest route to higher ground, Mullineaux said, not altogether reassuringly, but don't live in constant worry. "Living near a volcano is like driving a car," he said. "You know that some number of people each year get killed while in a car. But you fasten your seat belt—you do what you can."

Toutle's citizens relaxed some. "Before I came tonight, I was spooked," said Diana Wilbanks. "but after hearing him, I feel safe." Laughed another woman: "I'm gonna take my antiques out of their boxes."

But if Toutle residents were relieved, Spirit Lake property owners were becoming increasingly restless at being denied access to their cabins. They made plans for a caravan to protest the Spirit Lake Highway "red zone" roadblock. A group of 35 cabin owners, all wearing blue sweatshirts emblazoned with "I've got a piece of the rock," congregated in Toutle shortly before noon on Saturday, May 17. One member of the group had a sign on his white panel truck reading, "Dixy, let us go home." Law enforcement officials, anxious to avoid a confrontation, agreed to escort the protesters into their property.

While the volcano slept through the sunny afternoon, Skamania County Sheriff Bill Closner led the cabin owners and a handful of reporters to Spirit Lake, an exercise he described as "playing Russian roulette with the mountain." The cabin owners discovered their picture-postcard paradise had changed. Ash covered everything. Alder trees were strangely bare of foliage. Only a few skimpy leaves had budded out. "The alders are usually bloomed out by now," said Dwight Sutherland of Longview. "The ash is choking off the grass." The group went about emptying the cabins of valuables as a Washington State Patrol plane circled overhead ready to radio a warning if the mountain erupted.

But St. Helens, its northern flank now distended by 500 feet, was silent as the caravan made its way back toward the safety of the roadblock.

Not everything had been cleaned out of the cabins. Those who still had belongings to retrieve would have another chance, the sheriff's office said. Another escorted caravan was scheduled to go into the area at 10 a.m. the next day—Sunday, May 18.

*On May 17, one day before it blew,
the mountain's peak stands disfigured
by giant cracks, and covered with
streaks of ash sent up by previous
small eruptions.*

Sunday, May 18, 1980 8:32 a.m.

There was a stillness that morning unlike any other.

The sun had come up three hours earlier and the cold spring air was beginning to warm. The smell of Douglas fir hung in the air along the shores of Spirit Lake, a placid, glassy mirror for Mount St. Helens towering 6,500 feet above it to the south.

But the birds were silent.

Thirteen miles northwest of the peak, Bruce Nelson and his friends were beginning to stir. Breakfast would be ready soon. It had been a great weekend for camping, the best sunny and dry weekend of the year. It felt good.

They had deliberately camped well outside the area scientists said might be dangerous if the mountain were to erupt. There were others, though, closer to the mountain, inside the danger area. Some of them had permission to be there. David Johnston, the 30-year-old geologist who couldn't tear himself away from the peak, was one of them.

Another was Harry Truman, the 83-year-old widower who had remained at the lodge he'd run at Spirit Lake for 53 years. When officials told him to evacuate, he refused to budge, and accordingly had become something of a national hero. On coast-to-coast television he told America why: "No one knows more about this mountain than Harry," he boasted, "and it don't dare blow up on him."

There were still others—more scientists, and reporters and photographers. Watching.

There were many more in the area, however, without permission. Topographical maps, hastily marked with roadblocks, had enabled the curious to skirt around the signs and roadblocks. Over little-used logging roads they came, with their campers and their tents. They, too, were watching.

They would be frozen in death moments later, some with their arms folded across their chests, some with cameras to their eyes. Still watching.

It was 8:32 a.m. on May 18, 1980, and Mount St. Helens was exploding.

Seconds after a strong earthquake shook Mount St. Helens May 18, Keith Ronnholm, a geophysics student at the University of Washington, grabbed his camera to record this extraordinary sequence of photographs. Camped only 10 miles northeast of the volcano, Ronnholm's first photo (above) shows the north side of the peak beginning to collapse.

Following pages: The explosion grows, throwing huge projectiles thousands of feet (at right of photograph). To the photograph's left, the avalanche continues.

A strong earthquake rumbled through her, 5.1 on the Richter scale, the strongest since she had awakened March 20. Then more shocks, smaller, but continuous.

Suddenly, the northern face of the mountain, swollen and disfigured for nearly two months by pressure from magma and gases below, began to collapse. Jarred loose by the earthquakes, it slipped down the mountain's flanks.

At almost the same instant, a plume of steam shot from the summit. Within seconds, the cloud turned black, a horrifying, deathly mottled black, and roared into the sky.

The rock and ice cap that had been holding back pressure from the pent-up gases and magma in the core of the mountain was open. The fury was free. It was as if someone had shaken a bottle of champagne, tipped it on its side, and popped the cork.

Hot gas and ash and huge chunks of rock and ice catapulted from the weakened north face of the volcano. Shooting out of the side of the mountain, it was completely unexpected, something that had happened only once in the recorded history of volcanoes.

The blast was almost beyond comprehension, 500 times greater than the 20-kiloton atomic bomb that fell on Hiroshima, and it washed over the foothills and valleys beneath the mountain in the shape of a fan. In moments, it covered 150 square miles, leveling all that stood in its way.

Millions of 200-year-old fir trees that had graced St. Helens' northern vista were flattened, strewn like matchsticks, their bark scarred, branches stripped, entire forests lying like so many strands of an enormous wind-swept hairdo. Howling at nearly 200 miles an hour, the explosion tore some of the old giants out by their roots, throwing them up and over nearby ridges 1,500 feet high.

The top of the mountain went

Thirty seconds after the eruption, a roaring cloud of ash, rock and smoke envelops Mount St. Helens.

Eight minutes after the eruption, the gas and ash cloud has chased Ronnholm, at the wheel of his camper, three miles further north where (above) it looms over the fir trees, creating a surrealistic image of hell (right).

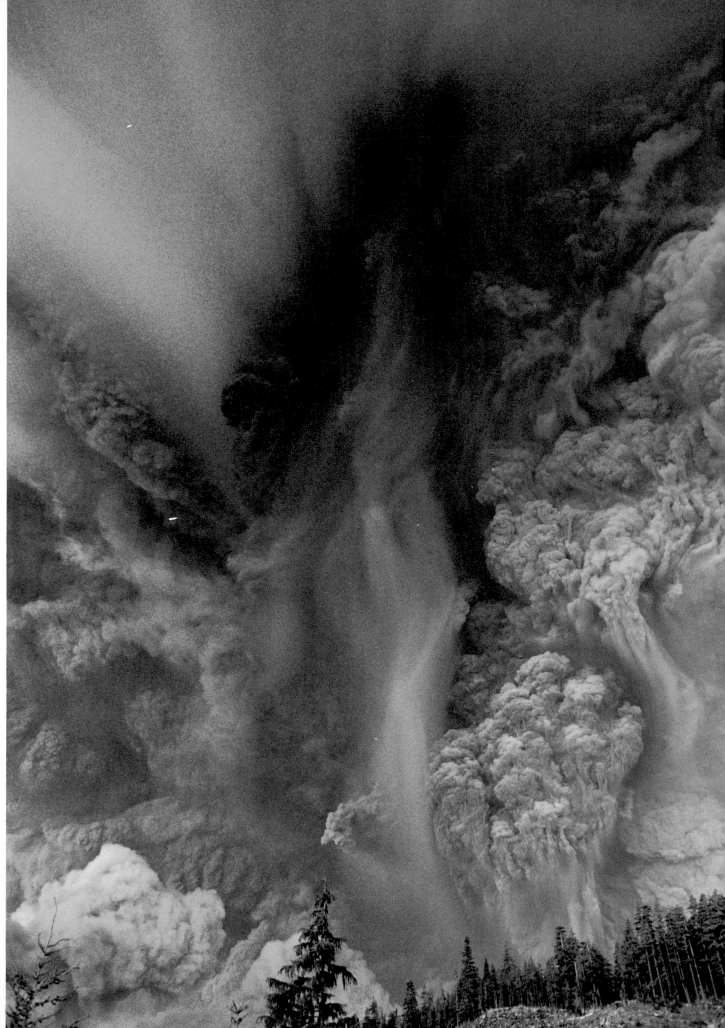

too, throwing 1,300 feet of the once-graceful and snow-covered cone, now pulverized, into the stratosphere. The growling black plume, laced with pink and purple sheets of lightning, shot 63,000 feet into the air in a pyrotechnic display that was to last all day.

Many of the people watching as the mountain exploded never knew what hit them. The mountain would never let some of them be found.

Moments after his exultant cry that Mount St. Helens was erupting, David Johnston vanished in a storm of hurricane winds and hot ash.

A geologist friend who landed there several days later told Johnston's parents the ridge, five miles north of the peak, had been wiped clean.

"The trees were gone," he said, "David's trailer, the jeep, everything was blown away." Johnston had been in the direct line of the blast.

Bruce Nelson saw the yellow and black cloud hurtling toward him.

He grabbed his girlfriend and they stood in each other's arms while trees crashed around them and ash nearly buried them. They were finally able to crawl to safety, but two of their friends died just a few feet away, their tent crushed in the wreckage.

On the fringes of the blast, some people had time, but little more than a few precious seconds to run for their cars as the cloud came at them.

Some of them survived. Careening madly down logging roads at 80 miles an hour, they drove, pursued by the spitting, curdling cloud of death. But many of them didn't make it. One man, standing atop his car, was taking pictures when the cloud enveloped him. Others, speeding from the scene, were simply overtaken at the wheel.

Mount St. Helens was reeling.

The avalanche that had become its north side poured west into the South Fork of the Toutle River, creating a new valley bottom with mud.

To the north, it slammed with even greater intensity into Spirit Lake, shoving millions of gallons of water down the lake's outlet, the North Fork of the Toutle River, and sending forth the first vast wall of water that was to rip into the valley below.

Where Harry Truman's lodge had been, there was now 40 feet of boiling mud. What little was left of Spirit Lake had become a seething cauldron of water, rocks, ice and trees. The trees were burning. Had anyone lived to see it, it must have looked prehistoric.

The avalanche poured on into the North Fork of the Toutle forming a dam of logs and mud and debris at the head of Spirit Lake, a dam that was to become 200 feet high and taper to the west, down the valley.

Mingling with melting glaciers and snow, the mudflow raced for the lowlands, destroying everything in its path, finally coming to a stop more than 17 miles from the mountain.

St. Helens' ash and smoke billowed to the northeast, crawling across the skies toward half a million people in Washington, Idaho and Montana, unaware in their cities and farms that they were about to have their daylight choked off.

To the north, 100 miles away in Seattle, and 200 miles away in Canada, few knew what was happening. Only a sharp series of explosions, like sonic booms, would give anyone an inkling of the horror Mount St. Helens had become.

From her innards poured hot ash and gas, the pyroclastic flows that had worried scientists the most. Roaring down her slopes at more than 100 miles an hour, they poured over the layers of debris already deposited by the explosion and the collapse of the north face of the mountain.

Joining with the waters of Spirit Lake and the melting snow and ice, the 800-degree-Farenheit flow transformed itself into superheated rivers of mud that began a journey of their own down both forks of the Toutle River and to the Cowlitz and Columbia rivers waiting below. It poured through two Weyerhaeuser Co. logging camps 12 miles away, flipping 100-ton trucks into the air, devouring a locomotive and emptying a storage yard of its thousands of logs, killing at least three people. The bodies and the wreckage became part of the mammoth chocolate-brown ooze as it raced on.

Twenty-three miles down the Toutle River, Roald Reitan and Venus Dergan sat up in their tent. The river woke them. It sounded different.

It was. Logs, mud, and by then parts of bridges and roadways were careening by, swelling the river to nearly three times its normal width.

The couple, camped near the river on a fishing trip, ran to their car. It wouldn't start. They scrambled on top of it, but it began slipping into the torrent and they fell in.

They clutched desperately for logs that had broken free from a dam momentarily created by a shattered railroad bridge.

Dergan slipped below the ooze several times, but Reitan pulled her out by the hair as they rode the wild logs.

Three-quarters of a mile down the river, they managed to wade ashore—injured, but safe.

To the north, the volcano's thick ash pushed on, too, borne along on winds blowing out of the south and west. Small towns 20 and 30 miles north of the mountain were inundated with the sand-like ash. Mount Rainier, 50 miles north, was blackened. Climbers on Mount Adams, 35 miles east, dodged charred pine cones and pumice falling with the ash, as static electricity danced off their ice picks. While residents on the south side of St. Helens escaped the destruction, they could only watch, startled, as the blackened mountain pumped ash clouds into the air.

The mountain was sending her message far and wide and plenty of people were getting that message. Rescue helicopters and squads of ground units headed up the Toutle to warn people living in the valley of the devastation rolling their way. There would be little time. The water and the mudflows were moving at speeds as high as 50 miles an hour. Many

people were plucked from the path of the onrushing mudflow and from other devastated areas around Mount St. Helens—nearly 150 during the hours after the blast.

But some refused to leave.

"I couldn't believe it," said one harried helicopter pilot afterward. "I told them what was coming and they just laughed and waved me away."

But the laughter turned to panic, as groups of valley residents who had left their homes and climbed up the valley walls watched the mud roll into their windows and doors.

It pushed right up to the town of Toutle, 25 miles from the peak, covering whatever was close to the river, but sparing many of the town's buildings higher up the slopes.

More than 1,000 people were eventually evacuated from the valley. Helicopters hauled out many of them, including those who had originally scorned offers of rescue. Others, who had more time, drove out in cars and trucks, part of convoys led by rescue vehicles. The mudflow chased them, wiping out 150 of their homes, flooding countless others.

Now more than a mile long, the mudflow pushed on. State police quickly closed the bridge over the Toutle River on Interstate 5, the major highway link between Seattle and Portland. They weren't sure whether it could stand the brunt of the debris racing toward it. The bridge held, but not before mud the consistency of wet cement salted with trees, cars, trucks, steel girders, sections of houses and animal carcasses swept beneath it and into the Cowlitz River.

By that afternoon, the Toutle River was steaming hot, 90 degrees. It flowed into the larger Cowlitz, raising its temperature into the 80's—enough to kill all its fish. It also raised the river channel in the Cowlitz by as much as 15 feet in some places. The 50,000 people living along its banks in the cities of Longview and Kelso began worrying about something new—floods.

From the Cowlitz, the mud and

Following pages: Its summit ripped open, St. Helens vents volcanic gas, ash and smoke into the stratosphere. On pages 34, 35, huge Douglas firs, knocked flat by the blast, litter the Toutle River Valley near Camp Baker.

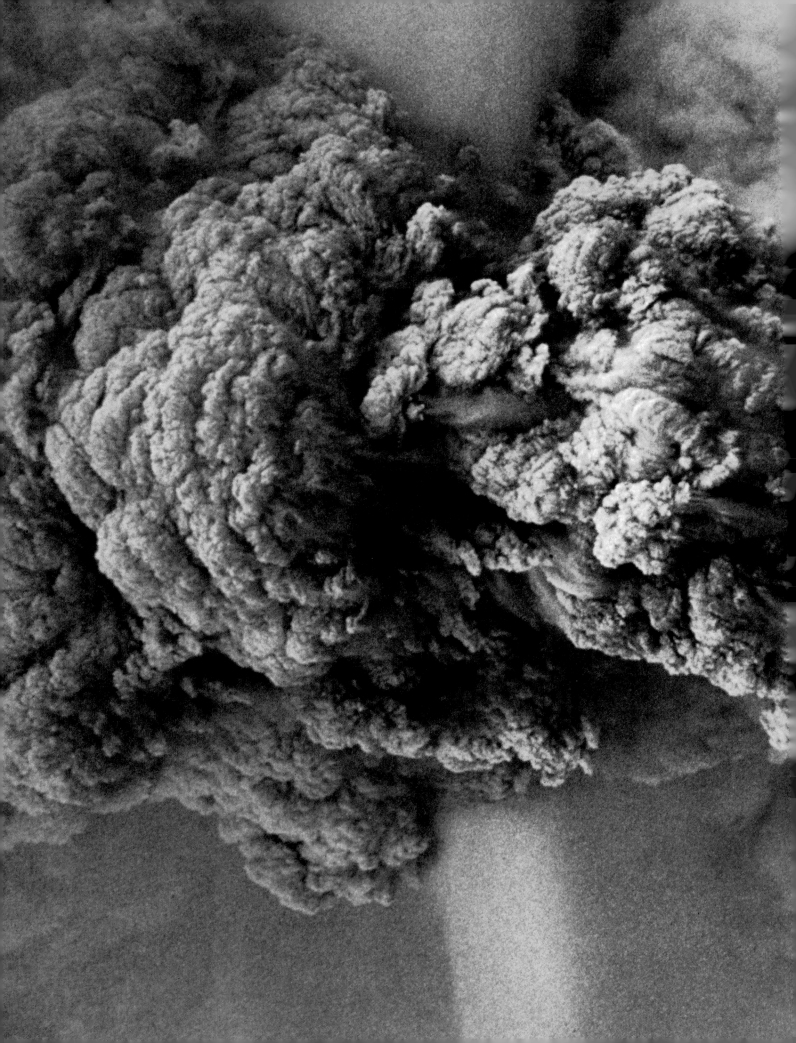

debris poured into the Columbia, second mightiest of the nation's rivers, and within 18 hours had shoaled its normal 40-foot channel to 14 feet. It built new sand bars and stranded freighters upriver in Portland, loaded and ready to head for foreign ports.

Ash had closed thousands of miles of roads in eastern Washington, bringing that part of the state to a standstill. Air traffic stopped, trains stopped, cars, buses and trucks stopped, their passengers stranded in strange places.

By nightfall, the mountain had calmed. The ash and gas that had turned Mount St. Helens' cone into a monstrous steam engine all day had quieted. Only a small plume hovered above it.

But the state hadn't calmed. Telephone lines were jammed as worried relatives tried to call each other. And there would be more worry the next day, for geologists were keeping a wary eye on the volcano-born dam that was holding back the new Spirit Lake. Afraid that it would break

and send a massive wall of water crashing down the Toutle River Valley, they warned the people living along the Cowlitz 40 miles to the west to be ready to run for higher ground.

The dam didn't break, but neither did the tension. Not for the families of the missing, nor for the 1,000 who had lost their homes, or the people who expected to lose their jobs. And certainly not for those living in the shadow of the awesome power.

It was only heightened when they finally learned the enormity of the blast that had torn the once-stately, 9,677-foot peak apart.

The mountain's blackened crater was now a mile wide and two miles long, its southern rim 8,400 feet high, its northern rim an astonishingly low 6,800 feet, nearly 3,000 feet *lower* than it had been seconds before the eruption. It looked, said one geologist, like a giant amphitheater tipped to the north, as if some huge hand had scooped out an entire side of the mountain, like a valley and two peaks where a single mountain

An enormous mass of steaming mud, the consistency of wet cement, boils down the Toutle River Valley (at far left, top). Above, it jumps the river's banks, menacing a farm home, having ravaged another (at left) from roof to cellar.

Battered by a 50 mph torrent of mud and fallen trees (top), this Spirit Lake Highway bridge across the North Fork of the Toutle River finally yields to the onslaught in this sequence of photos. The span bends (center) and is ripped from the banks and carried downstream (bottom), only to become part of the destructive flow (far right) it tried to resist.

38

Following pages: The 90° Toutle River steams in apparent frustration at a bridge still standing, on Highway 99 near Castle Rock.

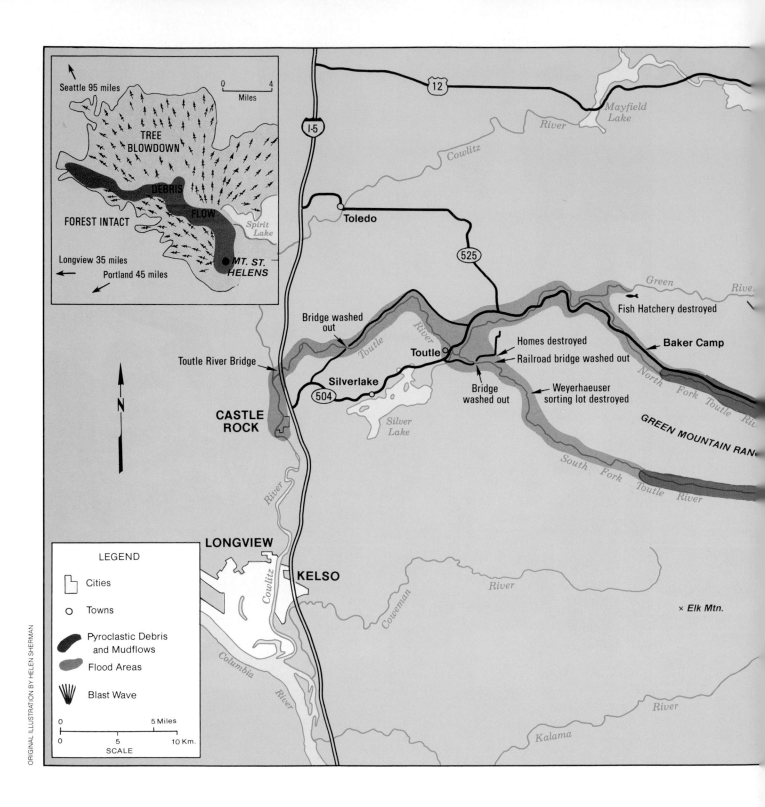

once stood.

More than a cubic mile of material—more than a ton of debris for every person on Earth—was thrown from the mountain, as much as had been rained on the cities of Pompeii and Herculaneum when Italy's Mount Vesuvius erupted in 79 A.D.

In the wake of Mount St. Hel-ens, nearly 70 people would perish (although the exact toll of victims buried under the mud may never be known for certain). Many of them died instantly, suffocating ash forced into their throats and lungs by the explosion. Some were burned to death. Others were buried by ash, mud and falling trees.

But perhaps the most frightening for those who survived was the possibility that it could happen again. They only knew that the mountain might not sleep again for years and that they would have to live with that. They knew, too, that Mount St. Helens had only taken seconds to change all their lives, forever.

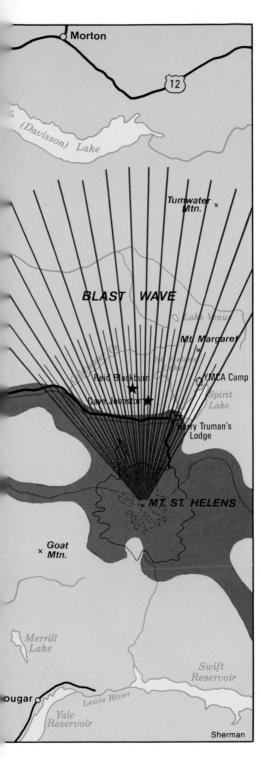

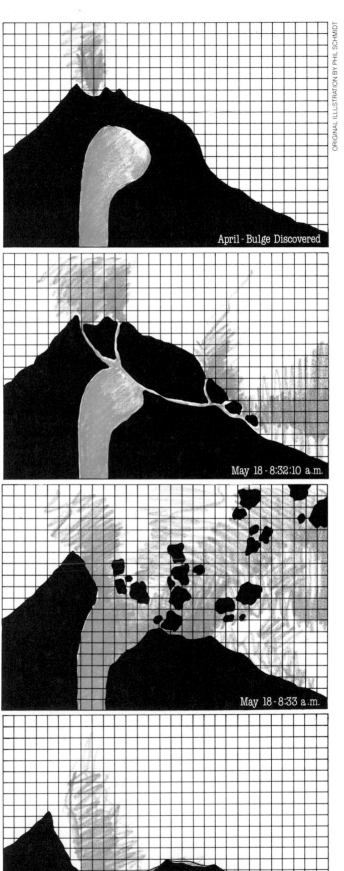

April - Bulge Discovered

May 18 - 8:32:10 a.m.

May 18 - 8:33 a.m.

Present Status

Map shows the far-reaching devastation wrought by Mount St. Helens. The blast area (in red) sustained the greatest damage. Mudflows washed down the volcano's flanks to flood the North and South Forks of the Toutle River (at left). Inset map shows the wide area where millions of trees were knocked flat by hurricane-force winds after the peak exploded.

In this diagram, pressure pushes up through St. Helen's core (top), creating the bulge on the north face. In the second frame, an earthquake fractures the bulge, and explosive forces propel fragments into the air (third frame). In the final frame, pyroclastic flows run down the shattered north face.

Clouds of Ash Roll East

Jim Barnes couldn't believe his eyes.

For 24 years he had been flying U-2 reconnaissance missions for NASA in the clear cold blue of the stratosphere. Now he was assigned to collect air samples in the great gray plume of erupting Mount St. Helens, and it extended up and up and up—all the way to 63,000 feet, where he had never seen a cloud before.

Jim Barnes was not the only person who could not believe his eyes that Sunday. Far below on the colorless ground that looked like Venus or Mars to him, people in Washington, Idaho and Montana were experiencing a day they would soon come to call Ash Sunday.

Midnight's darkness came at noon in Yakima, Washington, and soon the skies were black over Spokane, Lewiston, Idaho, and Missoula, Montana. The gritty cloud kept growing until it stretched, halfway across the country.

It was like an eclipse of the sun that lingered and a blinding blizzard—a frightful combination. Light-sensitive street lights came on automatically, traffic stopped, and a strange quiet fell. And everywhere the talcum-like gray powder kept piling up.

It brought wonder at first, then fear. "We were afraid that it wouldn't end, afraid that it would always be night," remembered Addie Anderson of North Bend, Washington. She and her husband Dave were driving back from a bowling tournament in Spokane, heading across the state on Interstate 90 when they saw the ominous black cloud. Soon they could only inch along the superhighway at less than five miles an hour. They pulled off the road at a restaurant in tiny Ritzville (population 1,940) and were trapped under five inches of ash for three days.

The Andersons were not alone. Stranded travelers doubled Ritzville's population—filling homes, the school and the Methodist Church, where they sang "This ash is your ash, this ash is my ash" to keep from going cabin crazy. Perhaps 10,000 travelers were trapped in three states.

All the machines that make modern America move ground to a halt in the ash. Airplanes, trains, buses and cars simply stopped; walking was all that worked. A region of the country that had often thought it felt isolated found out about real isolation. It was no longer possible to drive from Boston to Seattle on Interstate 90, nor was it possible to fly in or out of Spokane or scores of smaller airports.

Digging out from under the ash proved just as difficult as getting around in it. The stubborn substance clung to clothes, it formed little clouds following each footfall, it swirled up behind cars moving at even a crawl.

The health hazards of the ash were unclear at first. People were advised to wear surgical masks and supplies soon disap-

Facing page: In Richland, Wash., 140 miles east of St. Helens, ash clouds darken an eerie morning sky.

In Yakima, Wash., one of the state's hardest-hit cities, the ashfall sweeps the streets like winter snow, making walking a difficult chore (top, left). At left, two adventurous citizens stand in the middle of the city's main street, bathed at noon in streetlights. Some residents tried to keep the ash from their cars, but it kept falling, the water and mud making abstract designs in their driveways (above).

A scraper pushes ash from a Yakima roof (left), while a Wapato, Wash. farmer surveys the ashfall on grape vines (bottom, far left) and ash coats a county sheriff's car in Yakima (below). More than 50 patrol cars were immobilized by ash in eastern Washington.

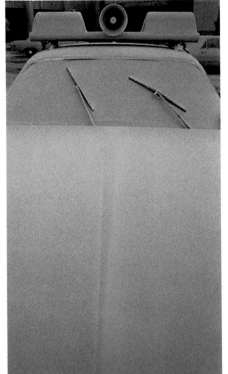

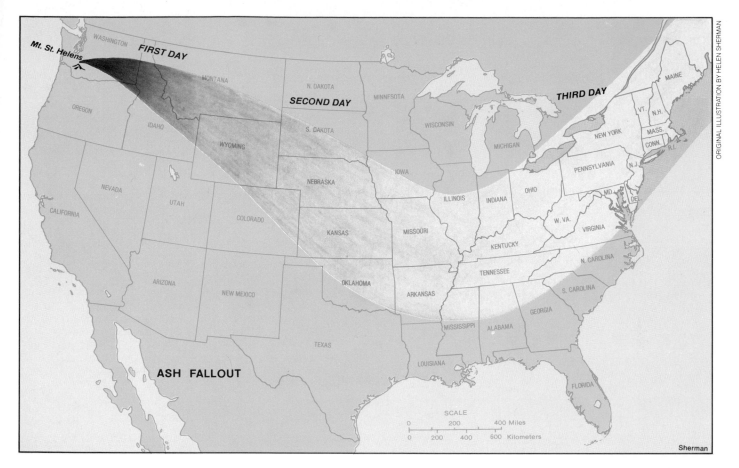

ORIGINAL ILLUSTRATION BY HELEN SHERMAN

Ash from St. Helens' eruption fans eastward across the country, dumping its heaviest loads in eastern Washington, and progressively lighter amounts across the country. Some ash will circle the globe for years, providing rich sunsets.

peared, even after 3-M Company diverted its entire supply of 1 million masks to Washington. Makeshift masks soon appeared — socks, bandanas, coffee filters secured with rubber bands. Soon virtually every face was covered, and a sign outside a bank in Yakima pleaded: "For security purposes, please remove your masks before entering."

Yakima was among the hardest hit. The central Washington farming community of 50,000 floundered under 800,000 tons of ash, blown by the wind 85 miles east from the volcano.

An emergency convoy of street sweepers and road graders was dispatched from Seattle, 140 miles away, which escaped the ash entirely. Grocery trucks went in convoy too, after receiving permission to travel roads closed to the public. When the massive washdown of Yakima streets finally got underway, the sewage treatment plant was shut down because of fears of permanent damage. Ten to 15 million gallons of raw sewage a day poured into the Yakima River.

Smaller ash-bound cities had little more success. Moscow, Idaho (population 15,300) dumped 15 million gallons of water on its streets and sidewalks, but with little effect. The 12-foot reservoir in nearby Potlatch, Idaho dropped three feet in one hour and was almost half emptied when only half the town's streets had been hosed down.

But as the ash was shoveled off the thoroughfares, the early fears began to dissipate. The ash was non-toxic and health hazards were not expected to linger. Farmers' frantic efforts to blow the ash from their fields and orchards were largely successful. The cleanup would take a long time, but it was not hopeless.

The most lingering effect away from Mount St. Helens will probably be a layer of ash that will circle the earth's atmosphere for at least two years. It will be a constant companion to Jim Barnes in his U-2, while on the ground it will provide people with brilliant bright sunsets — an ironically beautiful reminder of an ugly Sunday in May.

Entering Ground Zero

Where the clear river once flowed, a sickly green lake forms, dammed by the flows of mud and ash.

Muddy rivulets slice westward through the deserted North Toutle River Valley, now a dead and ravaged land.

Gray humps, the ghosts of once-lush hills, stand in the swath of destruction that fans north of Mount St. Helens. A pockmarked, lumpy mat of mud, miles wide and hundreds of feet deep in places, trails down a valley west of the mountain. Here and there, steam bubbles through. It was this way the day after the blast, and the month after. And it will look like this for quite some time to come.

On a helicopter ride over the volcano-scarred area, passengers sniff the odor of sulfur. At times it becomes a nauseating stench.

They call the land an alien moonscape, a blighted badlands. President Carter flew over it in late May and called it "indescribable." Dirty rivulets seem to flow uphill as they wind through the bizarre terrain.

At ground zero in the hellish landscape is what is left of Mount St. Helens. It sits like a resting monster, its egg-shaped crater gaping from one mile at its narrowest to two miles at its widest. The floor of the mile-deep crater is carpeted with ash and rock.

Several steam vents churn violently on the floor, and some water ponds are forming.

A National Guard pilot, Roger Kramer, returns from a flight over the new crater. "I'm no geologist," he says, "but I was scared bad. We could see stuff coming up out of that hole, and the crater started turning black, and there were small eruptions that began in an area maybe a quarter mile wide."

Chunks of rock break away from the crater's edge and roll into the volcano's mouth. Freshly fallen snow sticks strangely to the sides of the steaming mountain.

A logging company employee comes back from a flight of his own. "I used to know this country like the back of my hand," he says. "Now I can't find anything."

Above the steaming, moon-like landscape, a lone helicopter searches vainly for anything left alive.

Fumaroles, or steam vents, boil at the edge of what once was Spirit Lake, five miles from the mountain.

Near the remains of Spirit Lake, a newly-formed volcanic crater sits in an ominous silence.

Still smoking two days after the blast, St. Helens' broken summit dominates the land below.

After boiling down a once-wooded slope, this mudflow steams and gurgles, covered with ash and strewn with logs (bottom of photograph) along what remains of Spirit Lake's south shore.

Mount St. Helens exploded northward with heat and hurricane force winds that blasted out a wedge-shaped no-man's-land. What had been a forest is an ash-gray patch of stumps and fallen trees stretching eight miles from the volcano, and fanning out to a width of 15 miles. If you were able to walk among the downed, denuded trees, some of the trunks would come up past your chest.

Six miles northwest of the old summit and within the fan of devastation lies Spirit Lake—or what it has become. Thousands of fallen trees clog its surface. Streaks of gray-green water show along its northern shore.

The lake's west edge is blocked by a gargantuan mudflow, a mixture of ash and melted snow that raced west through the valley of the Toutle River's North Fork. Hundreds of tons of material in countless shades of gray and brown have dammed the lake's outlet into the Toutle, and one scientist predicts the lake will grow until it finds another outlet.

A coat of ash covers the ground around the mountain. It has cooled now, but was once warm enough to be felt through the leather work shoe of a man shuffling through it, a survivor of the eruption.

A few miles west of the mountain, out of the blast zone, a herd of elk grazes on a dusty hillside above the Toutle riverbed, as if nothing had happened.

But below the herd, a lone cow elk wanders aimlessly on the mud-covered valley floor. She is lost in a strange land.

Five miles from the mountaintop, craters 300-yards wide dot the denuded no-man's-land.

The gray and lifeless terrain of the
Toutle River Valley dwarfs a military
rescue helicopter.

"Don't Leave Me Here to Die"

It was Sunday morning in the quiet campground where Bruce Nelson and Sue Ruff had spent the night in a tent along the banks of the Green River.

Then came the volcanic blast, and in an instant, the two were buried in eight feet of fallen trees and ash so hot they could barely stand to touch it.

The initial blast had left them stunned, but alive. The trick now was to stay alive.

It would be hours before rescue helicopters, like the one at left, could reach the area, and days before they could land in parts of the volcano-scarred terrain. Survival became a terrifying ordeal for many who lived through the initial explosion.

When Nelson, 22, and Ruff, 21, dug themselves out, the volcano was pelting their campsite with chunks of rock and ice. They yelled for their friends Terry Crall and Karen Varner, another young couple, but there was no answer. Nelson and Ruff filtered out the falling ash by breathing through crude masks fashioned from their sweatshirts. In minutes, they found two other friends, Dan Balch and Bryan Thomas, whose hip had been broken. Thomas was too heavy to carry out, so the three others built him a makeshift lean-to for shelter.

"The whole time we were building the lean-to," Nelson said later, "Bryan was screaming, 'Don't leave me here! Don't leave me here to die!' It was a hard thing to do."

Nelson, Ruff and Balch, who was barefoot, started to walk out. Balch screamed as he ran through the hot ash and soon he too was left behind. Nelson and Ruff continued, and joined Grant Christensen, 59, whose pickup truck had been disabled by ash. It was three hours before they were able to signal rescue helicopters, using their clothing to stir up a cloud of dust. The choppers also rescued Thomas and Balch.

The five were among more than 190 survivors plucked from the area around the mountain in the days after the eruption. But by Wednesday, most of the searches turned up those who had not survived. It was depressing and mentally exhausting duty for Army, Air Force Reserve and National Guard troops.

Thursday, four days after the eruption, was the first day rescue helicopters could land in some areas. Until Wednesday's rain matted down the ash, the copter rotors would churn up blinding clouds as they neared the ground.

On one Thursday mission, an Army helicopter landed near an old mineshaft. Walking to the mine, the crew spotted a blue sleeping bag, two horse saddles and a makeshift lean-to. "There's a bag here with cooking utensils," helicopter pilot Charlie Wesler blurted into his radio microphone. "It's definitely been a recent camp. Someone's been here."

No one was found near the camp. Back in the air, the searchers spotted what looked like fresh footprints leading toward the camp from an abandoned van, and a pickup truck with a horse trailer. Four sets of tracks moved around the fallen trees.

Later, the air crew would learn that they were exploring the same area where ground searchers earlier had removed two bodies. But before returning to base, the helicopter would search longer and see more cars, more footprints, but no survivors. "God," pilot Steve Brooks said wearily, "I wish we would find just one person alive."

On that same Thursday, another helicopter flew in to recover the bodies of Terry Crall and Karen Varner. Bruce Nelson was on that return trip.

One of the first things the crew spotted when it landed was a dog pinned under a log, with three puppies around it. When the men freed the dog, it limped to the helicopter. Nelson put the puppies in his backpack for the trip back to safety.

Army personnel Von Roberts (above, left) and Pat Puhr search for bodies near the base of the volcano.

An Army searcher finds a saddle at a campsite, but no survivors. Two bodies were found there earlier.

It was supposed to be a nice weekend with the kids, their four-year-old's first camping trip. Instead, it was 24 hours of terror.

Mike and Lu Moore, of Castle Rock, with their daughters Bonnie Lu, 4, and Terra, 3 months, had camped near the Green River, 12 miles north of the mountain. They had parked their car and hiked up a gentle, two-and-one-half-mile slope of a forest trail Saturday, planning to spend one night and return home Sunday afternoon.

"We were up Sunday morning making breakfast," Mrs. Moore said. "The first thing I noticed was a rumbling noise. It felt like there was an earthquake inside you."

The family hurriedly stuffed their backpacks and moved to a nearby shelter for elk hunters.

"You could physically see the cloud of ash moving toward us," Moore recalled. "It was the blackest black I had ever seen." With the cloud came thunder and lightning. The family huddled in the shelter, breathing through socks to protect them from the ash.

Darkness was total for an hour or two—the Moores lost track of time. When it lifted, they made their way toward the car. Less than a mile down the trail, a swath of broken trees blocked their way. They decided to spend the night in their tent Sunday, and were spotted by a rescue helicopter Monday morning.

"Scared?" Mrs. Moore asked. "There really wasn't time. Perhaps the worst part of the whole affair was the helicopter ride out. I thought I might get airsick."

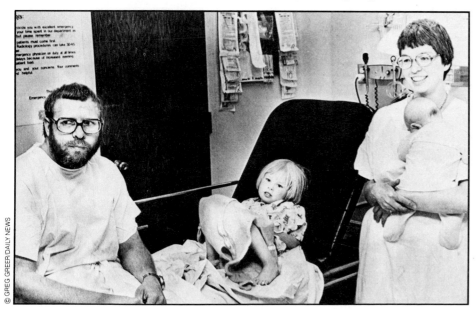

In a nearby hospital after their helicopter rescue, the Moore family manages a variety of relieved smiles.

In an attempt to rescue three horses stranded up to their bellies in the mud-mired Toutle River, John Brown (left) and his brother, Robert A. Brown, try to guide the animals over a stalled railroad train to the safety of the shore. The horses had been helpless in the rushing, gray torrent of silt about 40 yards from solid ground. The Browns managed to lead one horse out, but it ran back to join the other two. When a logjam just upstream broke, the Browns fled the rush of mud, and the horses were swept away by the current.

Television cameraman Crockett set these three signal
fires, which eventually attracted rescuers.

Dave Crockett doesn't know why he woke up in the middle of the night that Sunday morning, only that he felt something was about to happen.

So Crockett, 28, a Seattle television cameraman, loaded his gear in his car and drove off at 3 a.m. headed for Mount St. Helens.

By 8:30 that morning, he was on a logging road less than a mile west of the slumbering volcano.

He stopped the car. He got out. It was quiet.

Then the mountain blew. Black clouds roared into the air. A massive, turbulent plume, gray-black and laced with colors, raced down the valley, down the road—directly toward him. Behind him, the ridge seemed to explode in black clouds. He jumped into his car and gunned it down the road.

He spotted a road heading into a gully and up a ridge on the other side.

"I thought if I could just make it up there I would be safe," he said later. He never made it.

At the bottom of the gully, a bridge burst apart when it was hit by flowing mud and debris. Crockett slammed his car into reverse —then saw the forest behind him flattened. He was trapped.

He pulled his camera equipment from the car and started up a 2,000-foot ridge. Then the falling ash blacked out his world.

"I kept remembering all the things that happen during an eruption," he said. "The ash and gas, and the 2,000-degree heat. I kept waiting for it, wondering which one of those things would kill me."

He staggered toward a patch of

light and stumbled onto a logging road. The ash began to clear. He knelt in the road for a moment, and prayed.

Then, rising, he whirled toward the mountain, thrust both hands in the air, middle fingers extended, and yelled at the top of his lungs: "You didn't get me! You didn't get me! You didn't get me... Yet."

Crockett built signal fires on a ridge, hoping to attract helicopters. They came late in the day.

After his ordeal, relatives of people still missing in the volcano's aftermath would contact Crockett.

"You get a call from a father who wants to know about his son. What can I say? I tell them there's a chance. All you can do is keep praying."

For the offspring of Bill and Ellen Dill of Kirkland, Wash., each telephone call brought new frustrations, but no real hope.

Vigils

The scene was the same whether it was in Kelso or Kirkland, Washington, in Terre Haute, Indiana, or North Shore, California.

The living room was usually full of anxious relatives awaiting word on whether their loved ones had lived or died somewhere near Mount St. Helens. Frequently, the anxiety was needless; all that many families knew was that their relatives were visiting in Washington state, which included hundreds of people who were nowhere near the volcano's peril.

Every phone call tortured the tired relatives with a new jolt of suspense. Would this be the call, the one that would finally let them know for certain?

"If we'd just have a definite answer that they're all right," said Luann Dill, as she and her husband awaited word of his parents —Bill and Ellen Dill of Kirkland, "or that they're gone and just let it be over."

Sometimes the word would come and it would be wrong and that only made everything worse. Hal and Judy Bornstedt of Kelso heard twice that Judy's brother John Killian and his wife Chris had been found safe; both reports proved false.

Kim Pluard, 24, of Toledo, Washington, and his 10 brothers and sisters felt like puppets being dangled from a live wire. Twice they heard their parents, Jim and Kathleen Pluard, were safe, once they heard they might both be dead, and once they heard that only one was dead. This made the Pluard offspring so frustrated and angry that one child went up in a helicopter and two others took part in a ground search. Both

efforts were futile.

But the Pluards were luckier than some relatives. They at least had seen the volcano's devastation with their own eyes and knew how slim the chance of survival had been and how quickly death had probably come that Sunday morning.

Other relatives would never really know such things. They could only watch the TV film of the wasteland and read the newspaper stories saying the searches had been called off.

As rescue helicopters clattered into the Toutle Lake school, Goldie Vining and daughter Sherry feared the worst. Sherry's grandmother arrived safely on a later flight.

Taking Risks in a Deadly Zone

They were looking for a good story, some great film, a missing relative. They broke the law and defied nature to brave the deathly moonscape created by the mountain's fatal blast.

Don Crick was one of them. The 53-year-old independent logger ran a roadblock a few days after the eruption to look for his son-in-law and another man who were logging a few miles from the peak when it exploded. Tired of waiting for officials to search the area, Crick and the cousin of the other missing man drove up a logging road. When they reached the Forest Service roadblock, the guard on duty tried to stop them. "Go to hell," they yelled, and roared on through. When the ash on the road made it impassable, they abandoned their truck and started walking.

What should have been a five-hour trip took 23 hours, as the men hacked a trail through the maze of downed trees. When they reached tiny Elk Lake, where the two missing men were logging, they were stunned. The once-lush timber, some eight miles from the crater, was gone.

"Nothing was left," said a shaken Crick later. "It's like a huge vacuum just sucked everything out of there." A 110-foot logging tower lay flat on the ground. There was no sign of life.

The two searchers spent the night at the lake nearly freezing to death. Dressed in light clothes, they were not prepared for the snow storm that moved in.

Afterwards, Crick didn't regret his dangerous, futile effort, nor did he see much cause for worry at the prospect of a $1,000 fine and a year in jail, the maximum possible penalty were he charged and convicted. "I don't think there's a judge in the state or anybody else who would hang me," he said.

A Seattle filmmaker who took a crew of four into the blast area figured he got punishment enough when an ash eruption turned the filming expedition into what he called a "death march." Led by Otto Sieber, 42, the five had slogged through the ash for three days to film the destruction. On the second day, a National Guard helicopter spotted them from the air, but the film crew turned down the offer of a ride out. By that afternoon, they'd had enough, and when a sheriff's helicopter landed nearby, they asked to be lifted out. Instead, the deputy cited them for being in an unauthorized area, and flew off. "You guys walked in," Sieber quoted him as saying, "and you will damned well walk out."

Early the next morning, the volcano started to spew ash. "There was a rumble and flashes in the sky," Sieber said. "At that point, a helicopter ride began to look good." Then it started to rain, and the volcanic ash became like "syrup," two feet thick. "It took three persons all afternoon to scrounge enough wood to keep a fire going," Sieber said. Ash particles kept getting in their eyes, and by the time a third helicopter swooped down to rescue them the next afternoon, they had to be led aboard the copter by hand.

Sieber later admitted it had been foolish to enter the area, but tried to defend the purpose of his trek. "It's valid to risk my life and my crew's," he said, "to record this destruction firsthand for all time."

Two days after the mountain blew, 44-year-old San Francisco Examiner reporter Ivan Sharp had gone around a road block to "get a little closer to the mountain," but his car stalled on an ash-clogged logging road. When a military helicopter spotted him later that day, he agreed to be evacuated. But when the helicopter started to raise him in a sling hoist, the rotor wash kicked up a huge cloud of ash, and in the terrifying "white-out" that followed, Sharp was hauled into some tree limbs. He suffered bumps, bruises, a bloody nose, and a substantial case of professional embarrassment. Now a story himself, he told reporters: "I feel pretty stupid, really."

After a self-imposed "death march" through the ash, filmmaker Otto Sieber, above, faces the press. Facing page, top, reporter Ivan Sharp is hauled to safety following an aborted auto trip into the devastated area. Bottom, a weary Mike Gadwa turns away from a buried car, searching for traces of missing relatives. This lead proved false, and his journey on foot continued.

The Mayor in the Safari Suit, and Other Government Follies

There was heroism and heroics, hard work and selfless dedication in the wake of Mount St. Helens' eruption. Towns were evacuated, lives were saved, bodies were recovered.

But there were also moments when the helter-skelter efforts of governmental bureaucracies demonstrated that reacting to a volcano disaster was a new, and often confusing task. Long hours and bruised egos boiled forth, and there were harsh words and pointed fingers.

Initially, President Carter's two-day visit to the stricken area was beneficial. Local spirits were buoyed, and Carter's presence certified the event as a national disaster. His description of the scene on St. Helens was unusually graphic for a president: "The moon looks like a golf course," he said, "compared to what's up there."

But the president's presence on the disaster scene also seemed to do strange things to some people.

In the midst of an official briefing for Carter, Washington Governor Dixy Lee Ray interrupted, "This is all very interesting but the top priority is people."

Carter, taken aback, asked, "What do you need specifically?"

Ray responded with a spelling lesson: "M-O-N-E-Y."

"Well, goodbye," chimed in an angry Washington Senator Warren Magnuson, who has much to say about federal spending because of his post as chairman of the Senate Appropriations Committee.

The Senator and The Governor then launched into an impromptu version of "Family Feud"—arguing over who was a better budget balancer and who had less money to spend, while the president squirmed in his chair.

Carter had another odd experience when he visited an evacuation center. He stopped to chat at some length with a woman wearing a Red Cross jacket. She turned out to be a reporter for National Geographic magazine—the real Red Cross volunteers, who had been working at the center for days, were miffed.

The president was not the only person hearing conflicting reports. Citizens in the tiny town of Ritzville, Washington—one of the hardest hit by ash fallout—were first told to venture out wearing wet rags as makeshift masks. Then they were told dry rags were better, then they were told wet rags were better after all.

More serious communications problems also developed. Some rescue agencies tried to use phones and found all the lines

An informal—too informal, said some—Spokane mayor Ron Bair sits grimly between Washington's Sen. Warren Magnuson and Gov. Dixy Lee Ray, during President Carter's visit.

jammed. Other rescue units could not communicate for the first two days because of incompatible radio equipment.

Some humor did surface. Oregon Senator Mark Hatfield was stranded by the ashfall in Spokane when he was supposed to be in Seattle. Buses, trains and planes were not operating, but the enterprising Hatfield bought a supply of surgical masks, air filters and fan belts and then hailed a cab. His 300-mile, cross-state cab ride took seven hours. The fare was $415.

The problems wrought by President Carter's visit did not end when he left the state. Spokane Mayor Ron Bair was photographed meeting with the president while wearing an open-necked outfit. This informality offended some of his constituents, including Darrell Rosenkranz, owner of a Spokane auto junkyard. He penned a pointed letter to the editor that said, "Here was the mayor of Spokane dressed in a Safari Jim jungle suit. I couldn't believe he would meet the president that way." Rosenkranz enclosed $1 with his letter to start a "Mayor Bair Necktie Fund." The mayor, a former TV anchorman who prides himself on his appearance, defended his outfit, saying that he had chosen it because its color was close to ash and had not had time to change prior to meeting the president.

"I kept apologizing for my clothes but the president didn't mind," Bair said. "The president said my clothes looked very home towny, and he was fascinated by the dust on my boots."

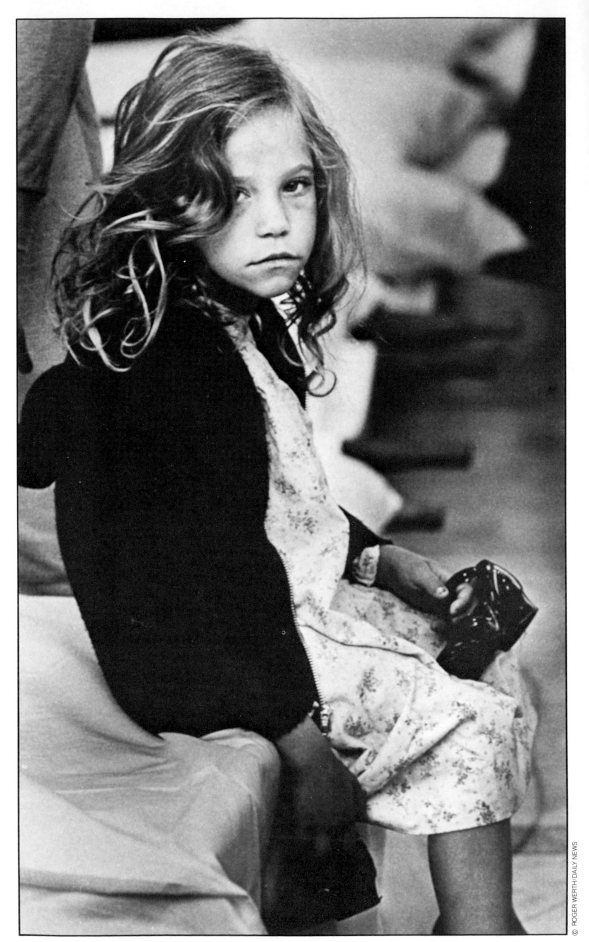

At a Longview education center, Kelly Presseisen waits —for meals, for President Carter and for her life to return to normal.

The Homeless and the Frightened

For once, some of Man Trieu's new American neighbors knew what she had gone through, half a world away. War had driven Trieu, 14, and her family from their homes in Vietnam to refugee camps in Malaysia. They eventually resettled in America, in Longview, Washington. Now they were refugees once again—from a volcano.

Man Trieu was one of a thousand persons in the shadow of Mount St. Helens who were evacuated after the eruption. Most stayed with friends or relatives. But about 200, including 30 Vietnamese, huddled in groups around cafeteria tables or on Army cots in the cavernous gymnasium of a Longview school used as an evacuation center.

They were refugees, forced from their homes by mudflows that shoved whole houses off foundations or by the peril of remaining in the lowlands near mud-clogged rivers.

"I lived in California for 38 years and never felt an earthquake," said Imogene Casey. "Since I moved here, it's flooded, snowed, hailed and stormed. Now a volcano."

The volcano had destroyed or badly damaged 300 homes. Nancy Althof and her family had fled to a hill near their three-bedroom home by the Toutle River. They watched as the mud swallowed their home. "Cars and trucks were floating by like toys," she said. "Then it was like the house was crushed. It crashed and that's all there was. It took maybe five minutes. We watched the houses of 10 neighbors go. It was awful."

Two days after the eruption, authorities let some residents briefly visit their homes near Toutle, a town 25 miles west of Mount St. Helens, to recover what belongings they could. Dick Schnebly stayed just long enough to help a friend pack and to get the car he was giving his son for a graduation present. "I've been through two wars," Schnebly said, "and I can fight someone. But I can't fight a mountain."

At the National Guard armory in Longview, troops helped unload the first of several truckloads of clothing and other goods donated to help volcano victims. Four days after the eruption, President Carter visited the school evacuation center. Most of the homeless had found other places to stay, and reporters outnumbered refugees during the president's stop.

For those still left at the school the mood seemed as washed out as the landscape outside. Red Cross volunteers walked between buildings, their faces covered with surgical-type dust masks. "I'm just waiting," Dorothe Cope sighed as she sat on a cot. "You don't see an end to it. There is no end to it."

On the South Fork of the Toutle River, victims salvage what they can from a mud-ravaged home.

© MICHAEL GOOD/JOURNAL AMERICAN

No Time
to Run,
No Place
to Hide

They could not resist the Siren Song of the mountain. They wanted to take family photos with its shape looming in the background. They wanted to camp in its shadow, hike its trails, sit around campfires surrounded by its trees. They chose to be close to an active volcano, and they paid for the privilege with their lives, becoming the first people to be killed by a volcano in the continental United States.

None had sought death, but some had courted it. Some had snuck around roadblocks, to be where they should not have been. But they still thought they were standing on safe ground, far enough away.

They weren't. The mountain unleashed a multi-megaton surprise that Sunday morning and their names were soon on a list in newspapers that many scanned for someone they might know.

They were loggers and lovers, families and fools, people in campers and cars and trucks that would be found buried by ash with all the windows blown away. Most died quickly, suffocated by ill winds blown from deep inside the earth and ash that clogged their lungs.

Very few were there because they had to be. There was a handful of tree planters and loggers, plus people like geologist David Johnston. And photographer Reid Blackburn.

He had been camped out watching Mount St. Helens for almost three weeks. Three days before the mountain blew, he had refused an offer of a few days off. This was just too great an assignment to give up—the stuff of Pulitzer Prizes perhaps—so Blackburn stayed put, even though he and his wife Fay had only been married nine short months. She understood what the mountain and the story meant to him.

Blackburn, 27, had been a staff photographer for the Vancouver (Washington) Columbian for five years and there had never been an assignment like this. He was out in the outdoors he loved and was working in a cooperative venture with National Geographic, the magazine that is the dream of so many photographers. They had two cameras set up—one at the campground seven miles north of the mountain and one at Spirit Lake—and they were making a photo record of the mountain's many moods with Blackburn activating the two cameras by radio control.

The National Geographic staff photographers were also on the assignment, but they had gone to Olympia for dinner Saturday night and had not returned. Blackburn was alone at the campsite, sitting in his Volvo sedan when the volcano blew.

Blackburn's death stunned his newspaper colleagues. He was

a quiet man with a wry sense of humor, the type who would put a funny note on the bulletin board and sign someone else's name. He was known for his sensitivity to his subjects and his commitment to his craft. He won many awards. When his body was found in his car, friends speculated that his remote cameras might still hold the ultimate shot of the eruption, taken in the instant before he died. He was the kind of photographer everyone knew would be shooting right to the end.

The Spirit Lake camera was found two weeks later. Miraculously, it was almost intact. It was apparent that some 70 frames had been taken, but when it was developed, not an image could be seen.

Taking pictures was important, too, to the Siebold family from Olympia. Ron, 41, was an avid photographer who took so much pride in his nature shots that he seldom seemed to find the time to take pictures of his photogenic family—wife Barbara, 33, and her two children, Michelle, 9, and Kevin, 7. The Siebolds had been married only 16 months, but they became a very close family in a short time, always doing things and going places together.

One of their favorite destinations was Mount St. Helens. They made regular trips to the mountain long before it became a big item on the national news, and they kept coming afterwards too. The Siebolds loved an old farm near the mountain; Jim had high hopes of being able to buy it someday.

That Sunday morning they were 12 miles away from the moun-

Photographer Reid Blackburn was found dead in his car, suffocated by the ash that had trapped him.

tain in their Chevy Blazer—plenty far away, the authorities thought. They were eight air miles outside the first roadblock. Their deaths were one of those events that made people stop and wonder. They were a picture-book family that did all the things families were supposed to do. Kevin was bright, Michelle was a Brownie and Barbara had begun doing volunteer work in special education. Ron was a loving father for children who were not his own.

The one solace friends could find was that the Siebolds had died just as they lived. Together.

Being together was just as important to Terry Crall and Karen Varner, two 21-year-olds from Kelso. They met at a party three years before—after Karen asked Terry to dance—and they were constant companions from then on. They often wore matching T-shirts, usually emblazoned with the name of some rock band, and they were both so tall and blond and goodlooking that they were often mistaken for twins.

"They were the most vivacious, outgoing, fun-loving, nature-loving people you'd ever meet," remembered friend Sue Ruff.

Terry and Karen had lived together for some time and had talked about getting married, perhaps in August. But their lives and their plans were always changing. Terry had been laid off for a month from his job at a

They lived together, they died in each other's arms; now Terry Crall will be buried next to Karen Varner.

Weyerhaeuser lumber mill. Karen was working as a receptionist at a doctor's office, but she wanted to return to community college and become a nurse. Whatever they decided to do, it was certain they would spend a lot of their time in the woods and a lot of it with a Portland rock band—both favorite things.

They were hiking with four friends all day Saturday, May 17. They camped near Green River, about 13 miles from the mountain. They had a great day; they had a great night. Dinner around the campfire was elk roast they brought in their packs, corn on the cob, baked potatoes.

The next morning, two of the friends were making Irish coffee when Terry slowly emerged from the tent he shared with Karen. He looked toward the mountain and shouted: "Wow! Look at the sky!" Then the giant fir trees started to fall all around them, and on them. Terry yelled Karen's name and dove back into the tent. It was buried by huge falling logs.

Capt. Jess Hagerman, an Army National Guard pilot, was a member of the rescue party that found Terry's and Karen's bodies four days later. "It was quite a compassionate scene," Hagerman said later. "He had obviously thrown his arm over her at the last minute."

Their four friends survived to see Terry and Karen buried side-by-side, in matching caskets.

The awesome force of Mount St. Helens' eruption resulted in bizarre death scenes on unearthly settings. Above, an Army National Guard pilot wades through ash on a barren hilltop eight miles north of the mountain where a camper sits, its two occupants frozen in death. Twelve miles west, a boy's body (left) lies in the bed of his father's pickup, tossed there by the hurricane-force winds. The bodies of his father and brother were found nearby, a tragic end to a weekend outing. In a cruel twist, the boy's mother first learned of the deaths when she saw this photograph in a local newspaper.

Vantage Points: Four Views of St. Helens

Some had waited patiently. Others got lucky—and had presence of mind. All had their cameras loaded, their eyes open and their shutters cocked.

And then it blew.

It had been 52 days since Mount St. Helens whistled its first seductive wisp of steam. We were told something could happen, but nobody was issuing a timetable. It could have happened at night. Or on a weekday, when amateur photographers would have been at their jobs.

But the cataclysm we would probably see just once in our lives took place just after 8:30 on a Sunday morning. The photographers whose works appear in this section were looking at the mountain from different angles. They all saw the event at the moment it happened. And through their photos, so can we.

Shortly after amateur photographer Vern Hodgson set up his camera 15 miles north of Mount St. Helens, it erupted, sending the entire north face sliding down its side (top). Then the mountain exploded with a low, ominous roar (middle). Hodgson changed to a wide-angle lens, and moments later photographed the mountain as it was engulfed in a huge, dark cloud (bottom). The white cloud toward the left of the frame is caused by moist air, trapped in the hot plume.

Darren Greenwood and Brian Hart, two cousins from Kelso, were driving back from the mountain that Sunday morning. Before dawn, they had driven up to Weyerhaeuser's Twelve Mile Camp on the South Fork of the Toutle River, arriving at 4:30 a.m. to take pictures. About 8 a.m. they remembered they had promised to help a relative move furniture that morning, so they started back. "On our way down the Spirit Lake Highway," Greenwood recalls, "we saw people pointing to the mountain. It was erupting." In the town of Toutle, they stopped and turned to look at the mountain. "We didn't know whether to take more pictures," said Greenwood, "or get the hell out of there." As the savage cloud blotted out the sun, they fired off this frame, then wisely chose to flee.

Cruising down Interstate 5 in search of a good spot to photograph the eruption, Martin Henry Kaplan of Seattle wasted little time when the mountain appeared. Driving in his convertible 35 miles west of the volcano near Castle Rock, Kaplan saw the cloud cover break and the scene at left emerged. Still at the wheel, he grabbed his camera and fired.

The 10 men and women and two teenage boys took a breather after climbing to the 11,800-foot false summit of Mount Adams Sunday morning.

David Larson, 14, leaned on his ice axe and looked to the west, toward Mount St. Helens 35 miles away. He saw a wisp of steam, and rubbed his eyes.

Smoke appeared, billowing larger by the second, and in minutes a black mushroom cloud engulfed the volcano. Jack Christiansen and Vince Larson, David's father, whipped their cameras toward the mountain and started shooting.

For 10 minutes they watched the black cloud. Then it moved toward them. Lightning flashed a metallic blue-white as it crackled from the thickest part of the cloud, still miles away. Some bolts hit the ground and others hung in the air for seconds.

"Listen, what's that sound?" David asked. It was a distinct buzz. Then the climbers realized it was coming from the metal heads of their ice axes. One man, holding a metal-handled axe, felt an electric jolt through his thick mitten. When another climber raised an axe, white sparks danced off the head and into the air.

The cloud grew thicker and blacker, and David said they'd better leave. "There's no place to go," Vince Larson replied. "Whatever's going to happen's going to happen."

As the cloud passed overhead, the sky turned an inky black. The only sliver of light was on the ho-

Seen from 11,800 feet up on sister volcano Mount Adams, Mount St. Helens (left) boils 35 miles away. The climbing party's base camp stands in clean snow at sundown Saturday (below), but wears a gray blanket of ash (bottom) after Sunday's blast.

rizon. It had been calm on the mountain, but now it got windy. The temperature had shot up 15 degrees since the eruption started.

A fine ash rained down, along with pebble-sized chunks, sticks and twigs. A five-foot tree branch fell near the party.

The worst of the storm lasted half an hour. The climbers held mittens, scarves and stocking hats to their faces as they plodded down the mountain, with the daylight slowly returning as the giant cloud headed east.

After a week's cleanup in Ritzville, Wash., a worker wearies of shoveling snow-like ash that won't melt.

With New Eruptions, A Dawning Awareness

David Johnston was right.

This was it.

Only it was a lot bigger, a lot more devastating and much deadlier than anyone, except for a handful of scientists, had suspected. What Mount St. Helens did to the people of Washington in her first hours of violent rebirth was staggering.

Nearly seventy people near the volcano were missing, many of them buried. Some may never be found. The eruption wrecked homes, bridges, businesses and roads, crops and machines. It clogged rivers and stopped oceanic shipping from a major international port.

It plunged residents of three states into mid-day darkness with its ash and then left them with a dingy gray powder that would stay on houses, sidewalks and roads—and in eyes and throats— for weeks.

It obliterated 26 lakes and damaged 27 others. A million and a half animals and birds died. Half a million fish were cooked to death in rivers heated to nearly 100 degrees. It blew down millions of trees. It would cost $2.7 billion for Washington to recover, its governor said. But somehow no figure seemed to fit the damage that looked so inestimable.

And perhaps the worst was yet to come. Mount St. Helens had turned on the people who had called her beautiful. A week after her first blast, she erupted again. It was a smaller eruption than the first, but it sent more ash into the skies. Only this time the winds drove the fury south and west, snowing ash on cities and towns that had escaped the heavy fall of the first blast. For the 50,000 citizens who lived in and around Longview and Kelso, almost literally in the mountain's shadow, the psychological impact was devastating. People there had lived with the anxiety of the first two months, the terror of the explosion, the frustration of searching for bodies, and the sadness of finding them. In the aftermath, there was the threat of massive flooding—sudden, if the remains of Spirit Lake were to break loose, chronic under the best circumstances, since the mudflows had effectively raised the river bottoms by as much as 12 feet. Now, a week after the blast, it was raining ashen mud in Longview. The frustration was palpable. It was their turn to choke. It was their turn to wake up to a morning where there was no sun.

Eighteen days later, there was a third eruption, this one lasting six hours and spewing ash 50,000 feet into the air. Most of it fell in southwest Washington and Northwest Oregon; more than an inch blanketed Portland.

But even east of the mountain where the ash had fallen the

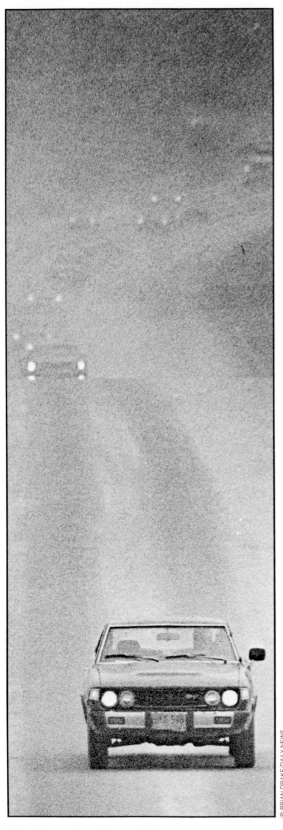

Near Olympia, swirling ash from a second eruption makes driving slow and risky on Interstate 5.

month before, there was no time to say "Now it's someone else's turn." High winds kicked up the gray dust that several cities had spent days cleaning up and churned it back into a granular, swirling fog. "Just when you're all piled up, your schools are open and your buses are running, she can do it to us again," said the assistant city manager of Yakima, as he watched his city's skies turn ashen gray for the second week in a row.

Throughout the rest of the Northwest, too, there was apprehension. No truck rumbled past but what people in Bremerton or Bellingham didn't stiffen, wondering if it was another earthquake's first shock. No dusty car went uninspected, a potential victim of imagined ashfall, no billowy cloud formation went unnoticed, lest it be another volcano letting loose. Rainier? Baker? Might they all blow up at once? Added to that was an unseasonably cold and rainy spring. Was the volcano affecting the weather? Meteorologists said no, but citizens weren't so certain.

People in the Northwest were beginning to realize they would have to live with a volcano that could disrupt their lives at will, at any moment. In fact, some scientists said it could easily belch smoke and ash and mud for 15 years— as it had in the 1800's. This was no short-lived act of God, like a flood or a storm. And it wasn't man-made. The citizens had absolutely no control over this mountain. They couldn't repair it, or regulate it, or shut it down, like a runaway nuclear plant. They couldn't legislate it, or vote it out of office, or even bomb it into submission. That thought alone was nearly impossible for many people to comprehend. They quizzed local radio talk show hosts: Why can't those scientists do something? Why can't they drill holes in the mountain and relieve the pressure? Why can't we dynamite it?

It was not an uncommon reaction, said the sociologists. People want control. They want security. That's why hundreds who were evacuated after the eruption wanted to go home, even when there wasn't anything to go home to. They had to cling to whatever it was that made them feel secure.

A week and a half after the first eruption, 45 Weyerhaeuser loggers returned to their Green Mountain lumber mill 25 miles from the mountain and right between two river valleys that had been ravaged by mudflows. The mill was untouched, but the loggers had no telephone, their railroad link had been knocked out, many of them had lost homes— everything. But they went back.

It's good for everybody, said the mill manager. It

shows we're going to stay here. "It puts a degree of normalcy back into my life," said the superintendent. "I think we all need that right now. Everything else is going spooky. We need something straight, something that's happening like you expect it to." They didn't want to think about the mountain erupting again. Or another mudflow.

And neither did their neighbors or the hundreds of thousands of others who lived in the Northwest with them. They just wanted the volcano to go away. People began to realize that what they had, too, could be unraveled within minutes or hours after another eruption.

The plush farming region in eastern Washington could be plagued for years with falling and blowing ash.

The cities where they lived—even "most livable" cities like Seattle and Portland—could suddenly become unpleasant, perhaps unbearable.

The machines that had rocketed man into the 20th century could be stopped cold by particles too tiny to be captured by intricate filters.

A civilization used to being in control, used to having an answer for every problem, could be thrown 123 years into the past.

With the comprehension, came an uneasiness about living with the consequences. "If this thing looks like it's going to carry on for 10 more years, there's no way I'm going to stick around," said a resident of the demolished Toutle River Valley below Mount St. Helens. "It's not worth it."

In Spokane, 250 miles east, what had been an adventure the first day was turning into a recurring nightmare. The ash wasn't going away. "You wash it off your porches, sidewalks and streets in the morning and by the afternoon it's back," said one resident. "My neighbor washes his car every couple days and it still looks like he drove it across the Sahara Desert." City officials told citizens the gray stuff might not be gone until the following winter. And even then they weren't sure.

"My bus driver's eyes are nearly swollen shut at night after driving behind cars that kick the ash up for eight hours," said the Spokane resident. "It's taking a human toll. People are worrying what the long-term effects on their health are going to be. What will happen to them if they breathe this stuff for 10 or 15 years? No one knows. I guess it doesn't mean life can't go on. But if the ash stays, there's a very real possibility that our lives could be changed and our quality of living could be changed for an extended period.

"This isn't a very pleasant place to live right now."

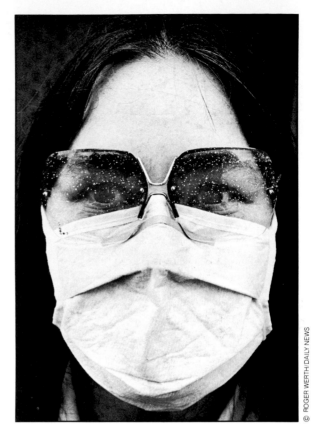

In Kelso the day of the second eruption, Liz Brailsford of Tacoma wears ash-covered glasses and a surgical mask. She, her husband and son had taken the train south to see St. Helens, which was hidden behind an ash cloud.

An Uncertain Volcanic Future

In the aftermath of the mountain's violence was the vexing question: why were the scientists not more accurately able to predict the eruption, and especially, the 10 to 50 megaton blast from St. Helens' north face?

Geology, as its practitioners are quick to point out, is a science, but an inexact one. Dealing as it does with things that are buried thousands of feet, sometimes miles underground, it involves a certain amount of guesswork.

There are several general rules in dealing with volcanoes, but the first one seems to be: volcanoes don't always follow the rules.

St. Helens was a classic example. As a rule, volcanoes blow upward, not sideways. St. Helens' lateral blast caught the scientists off guard, both figuratively and literally. Had they thought it might blow to the north side, geologist David Johnston would never have been where he was.

Based on St. Helens' history and what else is known about volcanoes in general, however, the scientists can make some predictions about the mountain's future.

Mount St. Helens, as a very young volcano, is still in its cone-building phase. The blast that blew the peak apart isn't likely to stop that process, despite the fact the mountain lost roughly 1,300 feet of its former 9,677-foot elevation. After a volcano ends its explosive phase (and most of the pent-up energy is usually expended with the first big blast), a lava dome—a thick plug of molten rock—often builds up to restore a destroyed peak to its former

St. Helens was a ghost of its former self the day before the May 18 eruption. But the volcano may rebuild its cone, possibly surpassing its original 9,677 feet. To the left in this photograph is Mount Rainier, also classified as a dormant volcano, and at 14,410 feet, the state's highest mountain.

height. Following an eruption in 1957, Mount Bezymianny in Eastern Siberia formed a dome that took a year to build.

More eruptions could send avalanches of rock and other fragmentary material, as well as lava flows, down St. Helens' flanks, all of which could add to the mountain's volume. And, as the historic record indicates, Mount St. Helens could continue its eruptive activity for years to come before returning to its dormant stage.

Does the awakening of St. Helens mean other Cascade peaks will follow suit? Scientists say not necessarily—although other Cascade volcanoes have been active in the recent past, and may act up in the future. Mount Lassen in northern California erupted in 1914, and remained ac-

tive for three years. Two Washington volcanoes classified as dormant—Baker and Rainier—ejected steam and rock fragments in the 1800s.

Besides St. Helens, the peak that most worries geologists is Mount Baker, near the Canadian border. It, too, is a relatively young volcano, and before its southern neighbor's spectacular 1980 blowout, achieved a degree of notoriety when it began spouting steam in 1975. Reservoirs were lowered and campgrounds closed by state officials worried about mudflows.

Officials in other parts of the country need not worry about such contingencies. The only active volcanoes in the continental U.S. are in the four Pacific Coast states, California, Oregon, Washington and Alaska.

Following pages: By late June, St. Helens had begun the rebuilding process, forming a bulging dome (the dark mottled shape in the middle of the photograph) in the center of the mile-wide crater. The dome, created by molten rock forced up through the crater floor, is hardened at its outer edges, but still growing inside. When this photograph was taken, the dome was 660 feet across, and 200 feet high—and gaining height at the rate of 20 feet a day. Geologists say that volcanoes such as St. Helens typically build and destroy such domes (occasionally by violent eruptions) until the pressures inside the mountain subside and the new cone becomes stable.

Harry Truman

Born: October 30, 1896

Died: May 18, 1980

The story was The Old Man and The Mountain. Harry Truman, the 83-year-old owner of Mount St. Helens Lodge, was a motherlode of quotes, the kind of character with all the makings of a media legend.

Truman sat in his rustic lodge with his 16 cats and his 1883 player piano, poured himself another Schenley's bourbon and Coke and defiantly dared the mountain to blow. It was only five miles away and it rattled his windows and shook his house, but Truman kept up his rambling reminiscences and his salty sayings for all who would listen, including the Today Show and The New York Times.

On the lists of the dead and missing, Harry Truman's was the name everyone knew. But many were left with unsettling feelings about how sorry they should feel for a man who refused to leave the volcano's shadow despite repeated threats to evict him and pleas that he flee.

What the instant interviews and all the snappy quotes could not quite capture was that Truman was a man trapped by his past. He spent 53 years beside the mountain carving his oasis out of the wilderness. He hiked all the trails. He knew the mountain as if it were a person. Besides, he had survived 100-mile-an-hour winds and winter's burying blizzards, and he could not imagine a sputtering volcano could be any worse.

That was why the last people who saw him alive the day before the eruption found him watering his lawn and getting ready for the summer's first visitors.

"He was an 83-year-old child at heart," recalled friend Jack Wolff of Portland. "Harry always lived for the future, he always felt a better day was coming."

Truman's long-time friends remember him, not as a cantankerous country coot, but as a complicated man. They remember an intelligent, well-read Harry Truman—a sensitive gentleman who hid behind the mask of meanness and toughness that he wore in public. "He'd throw you out of his place two or three times to see how you bounced before he became friendly," recalled Wolff.

Among those who received that Truman treatment was the late Supreme Court Justice William O. Douglas. Harry had thought the bearded man was just "some old bum" and sent him to another lodge until someone pointed out his mistake. Harry ran after Douglas and soon they were off on a five-day pack trip, where they became fast friends.

Most of all, his friends remember Truman's fond moments with

*The day before the mountain blew,
Harry Truman sat on the steps of the
Spirit Lake lodge he would not leave.*

his third wife Edie. She was a beautiful woman who brightened the lodge with flowers and complemented his feistiness with calm resolve. She knew when to stay quiet and when to kid Harry—like the time he mistakenly slashed his stomach instead of the sack of oats he was trying to open. "Truman," she said sarcastically, "you'll do anything to get attention." The next day, he rode 20 miles on a pack trip, then caught 17 trout at day's end, to prove how tough he really was.

In their 30 years of marriage, Harry and Edie spent long winters alone together in the lodge, and sometimes they took cross country trips in Harry's pink 1957 Cadillac Coup de Ville with the gold-plated wheels and the bar in the back seat.

Harry was devastated when Edie died in 1975. She was 13 years younger and he had always expected to be buried first. For months afterwards he could not play his juke box or his player piano because of painful memories of her, and he told friends later that he spent many nights alone in the lodge crying himself to sleep.

Four years later, the mountain's rumblings and the arrival of all the reporters finally gave him a new reason to live.

Truman's friends remain convinced that he died the way he would have wanted—with his beloved lodge and his cats and all his antique treasures taken with him, never to be seen by anyone again. And they believe crusty, but sentimental Harry Truman would have been horrified to see his Spirit Lake and Mount St. Helens turned into a dead gray wasteland.

"That would have finished him I'm sure," said Dr. Roy Peterson, Truman's friend and doctor. "He *was* Spirit Lake."

Truman's weathered face and salty comments got him plenty of media coverage, including this open-air press conference in the town of Toutle. "I trust the mountain," he told reporters. "I'm part of the mountain."

A confirmed cat lover, Truman had 16 of them to keep him company in the lodge (above). At left, Truman visits adoring school children in Salem, Ore. National Geographic magazine flew him there for a picture session four days before St. Helens' fatal eruption.

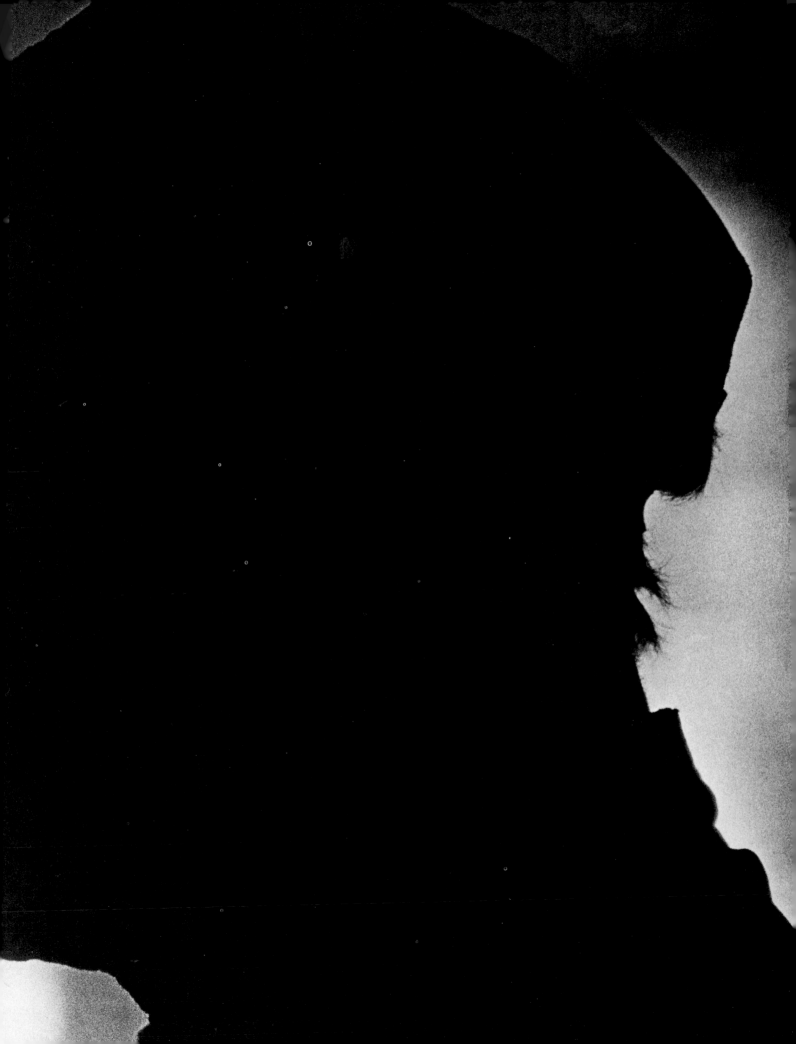

CHRONOLOGY OF EVENTS, 1980
Mount St. Helens Eruption

MARCH 20, 3:48 P.M.

Minor earthquake measuring 4.1 on Richter scale shakes the mountain.

MARCH 21-24

Series of "microquakes" recorded.

MARCH 24

Quakes registering 4.4 produces avalanches on mountain's north face.

MARCH 25

By afternoon, seismic activity has grown to the extent that individual earthquakes are indistinguishable.

MARCH 26

Federal, state and local officials meet to discuss possible evacuation plans.

MARCH 27, 12:36 P.M.

Loud boom heard, ash plume rises 7,000 feet above the summit.

2:01 P.M.—Earthquake measuring 4.5 recorded.

New crater formed measuring 200 to 250 feet in diameter and 150 deep. Cracks extending 3 miles to the summit.

Eight earthquakes recorded between magnitudes 3.4 to 4.5.

MARCH 28, 3 A.M.

Ash-and-steam plume rises more than mile into air above mountain. Nine quakes between 3.4 and 4.2 recorded in northwestern part. Avalanches of ash and snow.

MARCH 29

Second crater noticed 30 feet from first. Blue flames seen in both. Lightning bolts, some 2 miles long, flash above ash avalanches.

Thirteen quakes recorded, the maximum 4.2.

Scientists set up "tiltmeter" to measure swelling.

MARCH 30, 7:40 A.M.

New eruption blows cloud of ash and steam as far as Bend, Ore., 150 miles south.

Six more eruptions with ash clouds rising more than mile in air. Seven quakes ranging between 3.3 and 4.4.

APRIL 1

Strongest quakes to date, from 4.5 and 4.7.

In evening, first harmonic tremors noted, indication of magma moving underground.

APRIL 3

Strongest quake yet—4.8.

Gov. Ray declares state of emergency, National Guard called in to control sightseers.

APRIL 8

Craters merged by this point into one that eventually measures 1,700 feet across and 850 feet deep.

Longest eruption observed lasting from 8:22 a.m. to 2 p.m.

APRIL 10

Residents and workers return to area near mountain having signed disclaimer recognizing risk and assuming responsibility for own safety.

Upper north flank now bulges out by more than 320 feet.

LAST WEEK OF APRIL

Average of 33 earthquakes per day recorded measuring 3.0 or more.

APRIL 30

Scientists report bulge to be "most serious potential hazard posed by current volcanic activity."

Gov. Ray imposes restrictions limiting access within 10 miles of mountain.

MAY 5

Scientists confirm that molten rock pushing up inside mountain is causing bulge on north face.

MAY 7

Violent eruption after 16 days of relative calm.

MAY 8

Earthquake of 5.0 recorded.

"Seismic noise bursts" picked up by University of Washington scientists.

MAY 9, 12:01 A.M.

Second 5.0 earthquake recorded.

Geological Survey abandons observation camp at Timberline Camp, 4,300-foot level above Spirit Lake.

Al Eggers, University of Puget Sound geologist, says lava eruption possible on May 21 due to peak gravitational pull from sun and moon at that time.

MAY 12

Steam vents observed along crater's west rim.

A 5.0 quake sets off ice avalanche 800 feet wide sliding down 3,000 feet on north face.

MAY 15

Forty earthquakes recorded.

Spirit Lake property owners make plans to re-enter restricted area to recover belongings.

MAY 17

Twenty Spirit Lake property owners allowed into otherwise restricted area by special order from Gov. Ray. They were given four hours.

MAY 18, 10 seconds
past 8:32 A.M.

Earthquake measuring 5.1 dislodges north face of Mount St. Helens, subsequent volcanic blast continues throughout the day. Heavy ash cloud carried on westerly winds blankets parts of eastern Washington in matter of hours and continues around the world.

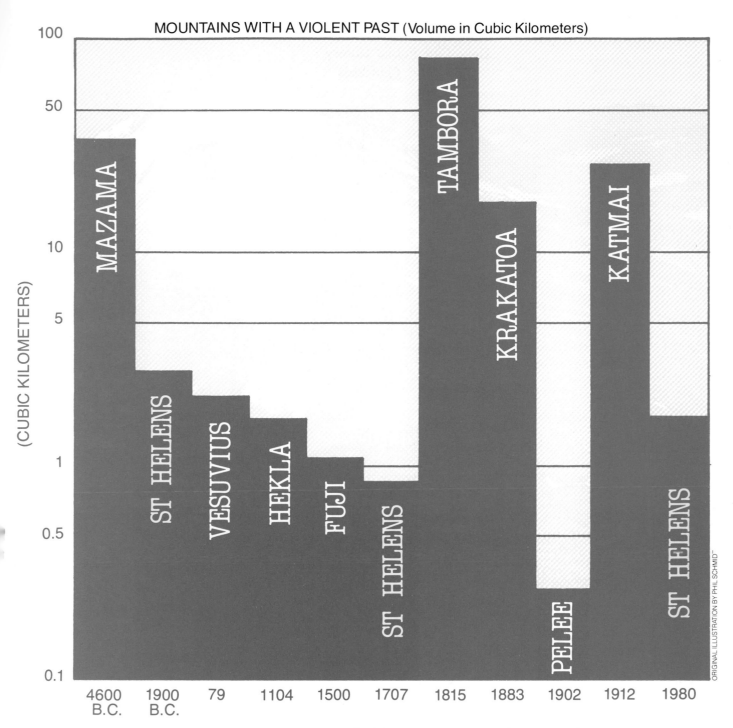

MOUNTAINS WITH A VIOLENT PAST (Volume in Cubic Kilometers)

(CUBIC KILOMETERS)

100

50

10

5

1

0.5

0.1

MAZAMA — ST HELENS — VESUVIUS — HEKLA — FUJI — ST HELENS — TAMBORA — KRAKATOA — PELEE — KATMAI — ST HELENS

| 4600 B.C. | 1900 B.C. | 79 | 1104 | 1500 | 1707 | 1815 | 1883 | 1902 | 1912 | 1980 |

ORIGINAL ILLUSTRATION BY PHIL SCHMID

Compared with other volcanoes, St. Helens ranks among the world's most active—and violent—mountains. Its eruption in 1900 B.C., was more spectacular than that of Vesuvius—although there is no evidence it claimed any human lives. The most deadly was Krakatoa, an Indonesian island which blew apart in 1883. The explosion plus the ensuing 130-foot tidal wave killed 36,000 men, women and children.

St. Helens' Eruptions Through History

Although historical records are not precise, it appears that St. Helens erupted several times before the birth of Christ, spewing forth huge clouds of ash, mudflows and pyroclastic flows. Typically, these occurred every 100 years, although much longer periods of quiet were also reported.

Geologists believe that in 100, A.D., there were large lava flows, and that in 200 A.D., and again in the mid 300's, there were pryoclastic eruptions, including considerable ashfall. The mountain was dormant for the next 1,000 years, except

for one pyroclastic episode in the mid 800's.

There is evidence that the mountain became more active in 1400, with lava flows and pyroclastic flows. This was repeated in the 1500's, and again in the mid 1600's.

The mountain was dormant through the 1700's, but in 1800 it erupted again, to be followed by the better-documented activity that lasted from 1842 through 1857. It was then considered a dormant volcano once again, until that afternoon on March 27, 1980.

ACKNOWLEDGMENTS

This book is based on information gathered by the Longview Publishing Co., Longview, Washington. It includes research, reporting, writing and photography of the Mount St. Helens volcano as published in *The Daily News* of Longview, and *The Journal-American*, Bellevue, Washington.

The editorial staff at *The Daily News* includes: David Connelly, Kathy Connelly, Brian Drake, Donna duBeth, Vince Evans, Stan Fagerstrom, Sheridan Fahnestock, Jan Fardell, Bob Gaston (Managing Editor), Greg Greer, Harriet Hansen, Virgil Hopkins, Ed Hislop, Fran Kaiser, Dorothy Krubeck, Jayne Little, Nancy Lundquist, Bob Martinson, Suzanne Martinson, Bud May, Dan McDonough, Jay McIntosh, Julie Mjelde, Ted Natt (Editor and Publisher), Tom Paulu, Dick Pollock, Lew Pumphrey, David Rorden, Jan St. Laurent, Rick Seifert, Lee Siegel, Richard Spiro, Andre Stepankowsky, Steve Twedt, Marlon Villa, Melissa Wallace, Roger Werth, Linda Wilson, Judy Wornick.

St. Helens coverage at *The Journal-American* included: Janet Brandt (Managing Editor), Dave Gering, Bob Goldstein, Michael Good, Sherry Grindeland, Jim Hallas, John Huether, Bruce Kitts, Susan Landgraf, Jeff Larsen, John Marshall, John McClelland, Jr. (Publisher and Editorial Chairman), Mike Merritt, Claudia Mitchell, Steve Miletich, Ken Olsen, John Perry, Frank Purdy, Ken Rosenthal, Cindy Schmidt, Terry Tazioli, Karl Thunemann, Sally Tonkin, Frank Wetzel (editor), Patricia Wren.

The editors would like to thank Richard F. Anderson, General Manager of *The Journal-American*, for the assistance of that newspaper's support services, and John M. McClelland, Jr., President of Longview Publishing Co., for his encouragement and support.

All of the writing and editing, as well as considerable original reporting has been provided by the editorial staff of this book.

Section Writers:

Jay McIntosh (*A Place of Beauty and Solace, Entering Ground Zero,* "*Don't Leave Me Here to Die,*" *The Homeless and the Frightened* and *Vantage Points*)

John Marshall (*Clouds of Ash Roll East, Vigils, No Time to Run, The Mayor in the Safari Suit* and *Harry Truman*)

David Rorden (*Born of Fire, The Mountain Stirs, Taking Risks in a Deadly Zone* and *An Uncertain Volcanic Future*)

Terry Tazioli (*A Briefing, Sunday May 18* and *A Dawning Awareness*)

Consulting Photographer:

Roger Werth

Art Direction:

For Madrona Publishers, William James; Barbara Haner.

Coordination and logistics:

Jeanne Martin, Cindy Jo Schmidt.

Proofreading:

Ada Lou Ross

Senior Editors:

Michael Good (Director of Photography), John S. Perry, Ken Rosenthal.

Editorial Director:

Sam A. Angeloff